£1·50

EXPLORING HERE & THERE

GLEANINGS OVER MANY YEARS

100 Sermon Starters & Devotional Studies

VOLUME I

JOHN PHILLIPS

AMBASSADOR-EMERALD INTERNATIONAL
GREENVILLE, SOUTH CAROLINA • BELFAST, NORTHERN IRELAND

Published by:
Ambassador-Emerald International
427 Wade Hampton Blvd.
Greenville, SC 29609 USA

and

Ambassador Productions
Ardenlee Street
Belfast, BT6 8QJ
Northern Ireland

www.emeraldhouse.com

Cover and internal design by Matt Donovan
Cover design © 2000 Grand Design

DEDICATION

I dedicate this book to Betty for whom these devotional studies were written.

When I was courting her Betty lived in California and I lived in North Carolina. Three thousand miles and three time zones stretched between. As a result, much of our courting was done on the telephone. In time I ran out of things to say!

I decided to write her a devotional every day. By the time I was finished I had written nearly three hundred of them.

Here they are, with her earnest desire that they might be as great a blessing to you as they have been to her.

John Phillips

CONTENTS

The Blood of Jesus
Hebrews 10:19

The Book of Hebrews tells of blood that "speaketh better things than that of Abel" (Heb. 12:24). Abel's blood cried aloud for PUNISHMENT. The Blood of Jesus cries aloud for PARDON.

The blood of Jesus was unique. No such blood ever flowed in other human veins though blood itself is unique in the complex chemistry of life. There are other fluids in the body—saliva, tears, gastric juices, and so on. But these are all <u>products</u> of the body. Blood is a <u>part</u> of the body—just as hands and hair are parts of the body. It contains both red and white cells and is constantly in motion. Each of the billions of blood cells in the body live for about 120 days, then dies and is replaced.

The chemistry of blood is extremely complex. Hemoglobin, alone, is made up of 3032 atoms of carbon, 4812 atoms of hydrogen, 780 atoms of nitrogen, 4 atoms of iron, 880 atoms of oxygen, and 12 atoms of sulphur—9520 atoms in all. Each of these atoms has to be hooked up to each of its neighbor atoms in exactly the right way. Such a substance couldn't "just happen."

Nowadays we classify blood by types. Before a blood transfusion can take place, the blood types of donor and recipient must match. Scientists now think that each person's blood type is as separate and distinctive from all others as are his fingerprints. Such is <u>human</u> blood, the life stream of the body, awesome in its function and its form.

Now think of Jesus, and <u>*His*</u> blood, for His blood is even more distinctive than ours. Our blood is tainted by sin, but His never was. His blood is immaculate. The essential fact of the Lord's birth is that He was virgin born, He had a human mother, but had no human father. Instead, the Holy Ghost came upon Mary; and the power of the Highest overshadowed her, ensuring that His blood, the blood of Jesus, was kept from contamination. Here is the important point—<u>the blood that flows in the arteries of a babe, developing in its mother's womb is not derived from its mother. The baby's blood is its own blood, produced within the body of the developing embryo. It is only after an embryo has been impregnated that it begins to develop blood. Every drop of a baby's blood is developed by the embryo</u>

1

itself. Since a baby in its mother's womb may have a different blood type altogether than its mother, the body sees to it that not one drop of blood ever passes from the mother to the child.

Jesus was virgin born. That means He had no drop of Joseph's blood in His veins and no drop of His mother's blood either. The blood that flowed in His veins was unique blood created by the direct action of the overshadowing Holy Spirit. It was sinless blood. It was shed blood. It is saving blood. And now, the Holy Spirit tell us, it is speaking blood. Abel's blood spoke, though only God could hear it. It demanded vengeance. It cried for retribution. It cried aloud for retribution, cried aloud from the dust of the earth. Cain the murderer became a stranger and a vagabond on the earth, haunted by the voice of his brother's blood.

The precious blood of Christ cries aloud too, for it too was shed by wicked men. It cries not for retribution, but for our redemption, and not from the ground but from glory, from the mercy seat above.

On the annual day of atonement the High Priest took the blood of the sacrifice into the holy of holies and sprinkled it on the mercy seat. The types of the Old Testament are as accurate as mathematics. What was done symbolically with the blood of the sacrifice has been done likewise with the blood of Christ. He took it to heaven and placed it on the true mercy seat (Heb. 9:11-28).

> *"Oh precious is the flow*
> *That washes white as snow,*
> *No other fount I know,*
> *NOTHING BUT THE BLOOD OF JESUS."*

BY HIS STRIPES WE ARE HEALED
ISAIAH 53:5

The healing of the body is part of the tidal wave of blessing that comes to us by way of the cross. Our resurrection bodies will be immune to sin and suffering. They will be like His glorious body, beyond the reach of disease, disaster, death and decay.

When He lived on earth, the Lord healed everyone who came His way. He never lost a case. He never charged a fee.

Can you imagine Jesus behaving like some modern "healers" do? Imagine Him saying: "Peter, you go on ahead into the city and rent the auditorium. Book it for seven nights. Matthew, you get some posters made: 'Famous Nazareth Healer in town for seven incredible nights.' Thomas, you take charge of the stage effects. Put up some crutches and display some testimonials. Nathanael, you take care of the healing line. Be sure to weed out the hard cases—and don't forget the hand signals we've agreed on. Andrew, you be in charge of catching those I knock over backwards. Judas, you be in charge of the offerings. We're really going to cash in this week. . . ." Why the very thought is contrary to everything we know of the Lord Jesus. Never, in our wildest dreams, could we imagine Him acting in any such way.

How did He do it then? Well, on one occasion He went to a local sanitorium (the Pool of Bethesda) and picked out the most hopeless case, a man who had suffered for 38 years. He healed him. On another occasion He cleaned up a small leper colony, healing all ten of the lepers at once. He broke up every funeral He ever attended by raising the dead—even a man who had been dead for days. The blind, the lame, the deaf, the dumb, the palsied, the leprous, the demon possessed, the dead!—there was no case too hard for Him. That was the kind of healing which was wrought by His LIFE, the healing of the body. Dr. Luke records an occasion when the Lord was surrounded by "a great multitude of people" who "came to hear Him and to be healed of their diseases." He "healed them all" Luke says (6:17-19). Matthew records a similar healing session and says that the healing Jesus gave so fully and freely fulfilled the prophecy of Isaiah (53:4).

The healing He brought by His DEATH, the healing which has continued on a global scale, from that day to this, is the healing of the soul. As the hymn puts it:

"There's not a friend like the lowly Jesus,
No not one, no not one;

None else can heal all the soul's diseases,
No not one, no not one."

The Lord's healing of both body and soul, (the healing of men's bodies during His life, and the healing of our souls by His death) does not exhaust Isaiah's words. The ultimate healing will take place at the rapture. In 1 Corinthians 15 we have a revelation of what our resurrection bodies will be like. They will forever defy the law of sin and death. We will be glorified and our bodies will be just like the resurrection body of Jesus. In our resurrection bodies we shall live on and on, forever and ever, in a tumult of bliss and full of that "joy unspeakable and full of glory" of which the Bible speaks (I Pet. 1:8).

Well, Isaiah, what do you think of that? You will share in it, too! You, too, will come bounding out of your grave, shouting along with us: "Oh death, where is thy sting? O grave, where is thy victory?" (1 Cor. 15:55).

HE WAS SEEN
1 CORINTHIANS 15:5-9

It has been said that the resurrection of Christ is the best proven fact in history, that there is more documentary evidence for the resurrection of Christ than for the conquest of Britain by Julius Caesar.

Something must have happened. There on Calvary's hill a Man died on a Roman cross amid the mocking of rulers and rabbis alike. He was alone, rejected of men and abandoned by God. But look now! That very same Man who was murdered, mocked and maligned is now worshipped by millions. Inside of fifty years, there was a church to His worship in every major city of the Roman empire. Something must have happened in between. Something did! He arose from the dead. The Man who hung upon that Roman cross rose in splendor from the tomb. "I have the keys," He says, "the keys of death and hell" (Rev. 1:18).

"He was seen," says Paul. Then he brings to our attention a body of competent and reliable eyewitnesses to that awesome event, witnesses whose testimony would stand up in any court of law in the civilized world.[1]

4

First, he was seen by His friends, by Peter and the other disciples. Take Peter, for instance. Something must have happened to make that coward brave. One day we see him cringing before a housemaid and denying with oaths and curses that He even knew the Lord. A month and a half later he is to be seen preaching Christ boldly in Jerusalem, charging the Jews with the murder of their Messiah. What happened? He met the risen Christ!

He was "seen of the twelve," Paul adds, referring to the Lord's disciples. They all saw Him together on more than one occasion. On one such occasion, doubting Thomas changed his mind forever, and owned the risen Christ as Lord and God.

Then, too, He was seen by the faithful. Paul mentions that He was seen by over 500 men at one time—most of whom he knew to be still alive when he wrote.

Moreover, He was seen by His family—in particular, by His skeptical and tough-minded brother, James. James had not believed the Lord's claims during His life, but he believed in them after he saw Him alive from the dead. James became a well-known figure in Jerusalem, on cordial terms with leading Jews and the acknowledged leader of the Jewish Christian community. The book he wrote testifies to the total commitment of James to Christ. He was given undeniable personal proof that Jesus was alive. That is what transformed him.

He was seen by His followers. "He was seen. . . of all the apostles," says Paul. One essential requirement, indeed, to be an apostle, was that the person had to have seen the risen Christ.

Finally, He was seen by His foe. "Last of all He was seen of me," said Paul. He once had been the bitterest enemy of both Christ and the church. He was converted on the Damascus road while actively involved in an enterprise to persecute believers in Christ. There he came face to face with the risen Lord and was instantly transformed and he became the greatest of all the apostles of the Christian church.

---

[1]See Simon Greenleaf. Simon Greenleaf was the Dean of the Harvard Law School in his day. He wrote a book on the laws of evidence which became a standard text for a century. He wrote another book in which he summoned the four evangelists into court and examined their testimony to Christ. His verdict—their testimony was true. See Simon Greenleaf, The Testimony of the Evangelists, Examined by The Rules of Evidence Administered in Courts of Justice, (Reprinted 1965 by Baker Book House Company, from the 1874 edition.

HE IS RISEN

MATTHEW 28:6

Here are the salient facts:

1. A man who claimed to be God was crucified on a skull-shaped hill called Calvary. He was certified dead by the Roman Centurion in charge. His death was accompanied by such awesome signs and wonders that His executioners owned Him to be the Son of God.

2. He was buried in a brand new tomb which was secured by a stone, a seal and by a detachment of soldiers. These precautions were taken by the authorities to ensure that nobody tampered with the tomb.

3. Three days later the tomb was empty. The stone was rolled back. The guards fled in terror. A visitor from another world proclaimed Him to be alive.

4. All through that day, and on into the weeks ahead, people saw Him alive.

Such are the facts. Either they are gloriously true, or else they are a collection of fables and fantasies.

Here are the arguments of those who deny the resurrection:

1. The first rumor to be circulated was that the disciples had stolen the body. To support this falsehood the Jewish Sanhedrin paid the soldiers who had reported the resurrection, "large money" to say that, while they slept, the disciples came and stole the body. This was obviously a lie. For one thing, the penalty in the Roman Army for sleeping on guard was death. If it had been true, that they had been asleep, the soldiers would have been the first to deny it. The Jewish authorities assured them: "We can bribe the Governor," they said. "You don't have to worry."

    But what a sorry lie it was! Imagine someone coming into a court of law and saying to the Judge and jury: "Your Honor, and mem-

6

bers of the jury, I consider myself a competent witness because when the events I have described happened, I was sound asleep!"

2. The second theory is that Christ did not really die. It is claimed He swooned on the cross, was hastily buried but revived in the cool of the tomb and managed to free Himself from His graveclothes. He then escaped into the night, and three days later showed Himself alive—thus giving rise to fables about His resurrection.

This view raises a multitude of problems. It assumes that a Roman soldier mistook a swooning man for a dead man. It assumes that the Lord's friends embalmed a living man when, surely, they of all people, would have noticed had He still been alive. It assumes, moreover, that the Lord's bitter enemies, who had moved heaven and earth to get Him crucified, would leave the scene of execution before making sure He was dead. The records declare, however, that the centurion took no chances. He ordered a soldier to stab Him to the heart with a spear to make quite sure He was dead.

He recovered and escaped, says this view. But, every bone in His body was out of joint; and He was fearfully wounded in both His hands and feet. Yet, according to this theory, He first unwound the graveclothes which bound Him, then rewound them, to give the impression that He had risen through them. He pushed back the heavy, sealed stone which barred His escape and eluded the guard. Then, contrary to all we know of His peerless character, He perpetrated a lie by pretending to have come back from the dead. This view makes no sense. It generates more problems than it solves.

3. The third view is that the disciples saw a ghost. He Himself, however effectively put the lie to that idea by sitting down in the upper room, in His resurrection body, where He not only ate a meal, but where He invited those present to handle Him.

Years ago a German pastor, known for his faith, was sneered at by a speaker at a giant rally of the Nazis in Berlin. "Pastor Schutez," said the speaker, "you are a fool. Fancy believing in a crucified, dead Jew!" The courageous pastor jumped to his feet. In resounding tones he said, "Yes sir, I should indeed be a fool if I believed in a crucified, dead Jew. But, Sir, <u>I believe in the living, risen Son of God</u>." So do we. There is all the difference in the world between the two.

PETER AND THE RESURRECTION
LUKE 24:34

With John, the impact of the resurrection was a matter of the mind. With Mary Magdelene, it was an affair of the heart. With Thomas, it was a question of the will. But with Peter, it was a matter of the conscience.

Peter had failed worse than any of the disciples. He had boasted of his superior loyalty to the Lord and then had denied Him with oaths and curses. The Lord had already dealt with Peter privately. Now, by the shore of Galilee He deals with him publicly. We see the Lord:

1. **Recalling Peter's Failure**

   Everything about the scene was intended to quicken Peter's conscience. For instance, there was the fire of coals to remind him of the courtyard of the High Priest's palace. There was the use of his old name—"Simon, son of Jonas." There was the thrice repeated challenge: "Lovest thou me," recalling Peter's three denials. There was the question of the fish—for God had called Peter to be "a fisher of men;" and, just last night, he had announced he was going back to his old fishing trade. All these things recalled Peter's failure.

2. **Rekindling Peter's Fervor**

   The Lord did hot harp, however, on the past. He never torments us with our failure. He deals with it, once and for all, so that it will never have to be raised again.

   We are all familiar with the play here on the two words for love.

"Do you <u>love</u> me, Peter?" the Lord said, "Do you love me with that highest, holiest form of love, with the love that is divine and deathless, spiritual and pure?"

"Lord," said Peter cautiously, conscious of his terrible fall: "Lord, You know I have a deep affection for you—a <u>brotherly</u> love for you."

"Do you love me, Peter?" the Lord said again, using the same high word for love as before. "Lord," said Peter, "You know I am very fond of You—I have a <u>brotherly</u> love for You."

Then the question was put to him again, only this time the Lord used Peter's word: "Are you fond of me?" He asked. Peter was broken. "Lord, you know. You know I can never love you the way you love me. But you know my heart. You know I have a <u>brotherly</u> love for you—a warm, and human kind of love."

3.   **Reshaping Peter's Future**

"Then feed my lambs," Jesus said. "Feed my sheep. Feed the flock of God." Peter, I have already given you an evangelistic ministry. I have called you to be a fisher of men. Now I am also going to give you a pastoral ministry. I want you to take care of the flock of God.

"Oh, and by the way, Peter, there's something more. I not only want to draw your attention to the <u>fish</u>, and to the <u>flock</u>, I also want to draw your attention to the <u>foe</u>. I told you once before that Satan desired to have you to sift you as wheat. Well, he still wants you. He will attack you when you are old. You will be put to death for me. You will be crucified. And this time, Peter, there will be no fall. I have recalled your failure and I have rekindled your fervor for one reason only—so that I can reshape your future."

<u>That</u> is ever His goal.

THOMAS AND THE RESURRECTION
JOHN 20:24-29

It was not so much the <u>mind</u> of Thomas that had to be captured, skeptic that he was, before he could believe in the resurrection. With <u>John</u> it was a matter of the mind. Nor was it so much a matter of the <u>heart</u> as it was with Mary. With Thomas it was a matter of the <u>will</u>. "I <u>will</u> not believe!" he said. Those were his very own words.

But let us back up. The day of the resurrection was over. What a day it had been! We can imagine the confusion and consternation which reigned in the ranks of God's enemies. What, we wonder, did Pilate say to his wife when news of Christ's resurrection came filtering in? And there could not have been much mocking now by Herod and his men of war. As for Caiaphas and his gang of renegade priests, well might they stare at one another in silent dismay. Not that they took it lying down. It was in keeping with their determined unbelief that they should forge and foist a lie upon the world. Just the same, the truth was that Jesus was alive from the dead. Well may they tremble in their secret souls. What kind of vengeance would He deal out to them?

But in that blessed upper room, it had been a foretaste of glory. Jesus had come in through the wall! He had shown the disciples His hands and His side. He had sat down to table and eaten a meal. Then He had vanished from their sight. He was <u>alive</u>! Alive to die no more! Whether they could see Him or not, He was alive!

And poor Thomas had not been there! Doubtless he had his excuses— "That upper room is a dangerous place just now," he might have said to himself. "And the meetings are boring these days. No doubt Simon Peter will be throwing his weight around. Besides, it looks like rain!" In the end he went to the gathering but, when he did finally show up, it was all over. He'd missed it! The others tried to tell him—Jesus had come! He dug in his heels. "I will not believe," he said, "I want proof, hard, tangible proof."

But we know this—Thomas was there the next Sunday! Perhaps he remembered the simple rule for gathering which Jesus had laid down—

"Where two or three are gathered together in My Name, there am I in the midst of them." He made up his mind to be there.

And it happened again, just as before. All of a sudden, Jesus was there in the midst. And, there was Thomas in his usual seat. Up to the startling moment of truth we can picture the stubborn set of his shoulders, the scornful look on his face, the fixed jut of his jaw.

But that jaw dropped in a hurry. For there was Jesus smiling at him across the room. "Thomas," He said, "come over here. Let me have your finger—put in into the nail prints if that's what it takes. Give me your hand. Come and put it into my side."

"My Lord! My God!" cried Thomas, his will broken, and his heart broken, too. "My Lord!" That put Jesus on the throne of his heart. "My God!" That put Jesus on the throne of the universe.

"Well, Thomas," Jesus said, "you have seen and believed. But blessed are those who have not seen, and yet have believed." Surely the Lord had us in mind. We have not seen—but we have believed. "Blessed art thou!" He says, "Blessed art thou."

MARY MAGDALENE AND THE RESURRECTION
JOHN 20:1-2, 11-18

She had already been to the tome and found it open and empty, and she had found Peter and John and told them the tale. They left her standing in a cloud of dust as they raced each other to the tomb. Slowly she wended her way back, drawn as by a magnet to that opened sepulcher.

We note her distress. There had been some coming and going; but all that was past, and now Mary stood there alone. "She stood at the sepulcher weeping," John says. The word for weeping, the same one used of Mary of Bethany when she went to meet Jesus at Lazarus' tomb, literally means "to wail." For Mary of Magdala was desolated, her only thought was that someone had broken into the tomb and stolen the body. Who could have done such a thing? The Sanhedrin, perhaps, determined to wreak their wrath on the human clay of the Christ of God by dumping the body in a criminal's grave or, worse still, in the fires of the valley of Gehenna. She wept.

We note also her <u>discovery</u>. She did what John had done. She stooped down to peer inside the tomb. And, behold, it was empty no more! Two angels had come, and one was sitting where the head had been, the other where the feet had been. Perhaps it was Gabriel, the messenger angel and Michael, the martial angel.

By this time all Jerusalem and all Judea should have been crowding to that empty tomb to view the evidence that it bore to a resurrected Christ. The only ones who came were two messengers from another world, and one lone, weeping woman from this one.

We note next her <u>disinterest</u>. She turned her back on the angels. It was not angels she wanted, it was Jesus. Her disinterest in them must have astonished them. Usually, when they appeared, people trembled, stood and stared, or fell flat on the floor. No one had ever ignored them before.

And, standing there in the shadows, delighted at such single-hearted love, was Jesus. For no sooner did Mary turn from the angels than she saw Him.

Note, also, her <u>despair</u>. She did not recognize the One who now caught and held her eye. She supposed He was the gardener. He was, of course! He it was, long centuries before, who had planted a garden eastward in Eden as a home for Adam and Eve. "Are you the one who has taken the body?" she said. "Please tell me where He is. I want Him. I love Him. I'll take Him away." There was not much <u>logic</u> in that—but there was a whole lot of love.

Finally we see her <u>delight</u>. The Lord could contain Himself no longer. Here was love stronger than death, love that many waters could not quench. "Mary!" He said. "Master!" she replied. One word, answered by one word. Often love needs no words. Here two words said it all. "Mary!" "Master!"

She would have clung to Him. But He said, "Touch me not. There are things I have to do. I must go to My Father. And there are things you have to do. You must go and tell My disciples I am alive and will meet them soon in Galilee."

And so she did and thus became the first evangelist of the gospel age.

JESUS IN THE MIDST
MATTHEW 18:20

In the midst! That is where He belongs, at the center of things. Here are some occasions when we see Him in the midst.

We see Him, first, in the midst of the curious rabbis of Jerusalem. They did not know who He was. All they saw was a thoughtful boy, and they were used to thoughtful boys. They had been thoughtful boys once themselves.

These men were the descendants and the spiritual heirs of the handful of those Jews who had come back from Babylon fired by thoughts of a building and a book. But it was the book that dominated their lives once the building, a temple for their God, was up. They began to tinker with the book until, in time, their commentaries and traditions became the Talmud. Even in its earliest forms it all but replaced God's word in their thoughts. Now, in their midst, in fashion as a boy, stood one who was none other than the Author of the Book, the Divine Lawgiver of Sinai. He sat there among them, "both hearing them and asking them questions;" and they knew Him not. How sad! To read the Bible, and not to know the very One it is all about.

We see Him, too, in the midst of the crucified robbers at Calvary. Hardly anyone seemed to know just who He was. Caiaphas looked at Him and saw a menacing problem. "We'll just have to get rid of Him," he said, "or He'll start a war with Rome and we'll lose our authority and power."

Herod looked at Him and saw a miserable preacher. He had heard of Him from afar. He had his own views as to who He was. He hoped to see Him perform a miracle, a clever piece of magic. He questioned Him eagerly. All he received back was a stony silence. Jesus had nothing to say to this godless man, the man who had murdered His friend. He was enraged and began to cover Him with abuse. The man who had murdered John now mocked at Jesus.

Pilate looked at Him and saw a misguided pretender, One who claimed to be the King of the Jews. Pilate knew what Caesar expected him to do with rival kings. He must crucify them—so, off to Calvary with Him, in the fitting company of a couple of thieves! And, wonder of wonders, one of those thieves figured it out. This Man in the midst was the Messiah himself; at once he owned Him to be both Savior and Lord.

Finally, we see Him in the midst of the <u>crowned royalties of heaven</u>. John, caught up into heaven, had trouble finding Him at first. He had been so taken up with the sights and sounds of glory that he failed to see the Lord. But, there He was, in the midst—in the midst of the throne and of the chanting cherubim and of the adoring elders.

But there is one more thought. Today He is in the midst of the <u>converted remnant of earth</u>—"Where two or three are gathered together in My Name," He says, "there am I in the midst of them!" (Matt. 18:20) But all too often we fail to see Him. The hymnwritier says:

> *"If now with eyes defiled and dim,*
> *We see the signs but see not Him,*
> *Oh may His love the scales displace,*
> *And bid us see Him face to face."*

THE MYSTERY OF GODLINESS
I TIMOTHY 3:16

"Great is the mystery," said the inspired apostle, "God was manifest in flesh." First there was <u>A Plan Rooted In Eternity</u>. The plan was made before ever time began, before ever the rustle of an angel's wing disturbed the silence of eternity. It was made before ever the "mystery of iniquity" raised its head in the universe and before "the mystery of godliness" was conceived—the great plan of God to make guilty people godly. That plan was rooted in eternity. Thus Jesus is "The Lamb slain from <u>before</u> the foundation of the world" (Rev. 13:8)

Next there was <u>A Place Rooted On Earth</u>. God, in His wisdom, chose our planet to be the place where He would deal with the sin question when it raised its head in the universe. He would send His own Son, to Earth, a tiny planet circling an insignificant sun, 30,000 light years from the center of a distant galaxy of a 100 billion stars. And having chosen this planet to

14

be the place, He picked a remote and insignificant town in a small and unimportant province to be the place. Not glorious Athens, home of a thousand thinkers, not imperial Rome, home of countless legions, not favored Jerusalem, home of a long line of illustrious kings—but Bethlehem, hidden among the hills, away from the rush and roar of the world. A place!

Then, too, there was <u>A Path Rooted In Scripture</u>. For once "the mystery" took form, and God was manifest in flesh, He followed a predetermined path from a cradle, humble beyond anything which could have been imagined, to a death, horrendous, too, beyond anything imagined. And that predetermined path was spelled out in the library of thirty nine Spirit-inspired books which made up the Old Testament. His birth, His life, His character, His death, His tomb, His resurrection—all was foreknown and foretold. No other person on this planet has had his coming character and career so amazingly foretold. When Herod heard from the wise men that the Messiah had been born, he appealed at once to the rabbis he kept at court—"And where is this one to be born?" he demanded. The answer came fast enough—"Bethlehem," they said. Bethlehem was to be the place where God would be manifest in flesh.

And so it was, for the Scripture cannot be broken. Herod, evil, guilt-ridden, crime-haunted man that he was, tried to murder the newborn Christ. He failed. So, the mystery of making people godly had begun. And there is another part of the mystery, as penned by Giles Fletcher.[1]

> *"A Child He was, and had not learned to speak*
> *Who with His words the world before did make;*
> *A mother's arms Him bare, He was so weak*
> *Who with His hands the vault of heaven could shake,*
> *See how small room my infant Lord doth take*
> *Whom all the world is not enough to hold."*

So the mystery of iniquity invaded our planet, brought by fallen Lucifer, hell's gift to earth. And now the mystery of godliness has come, brought by God the Son, no less—heaven's gift to men. And so we have to choose sides. Who but a fool would find it hard to decide which one to choose?

---

[1]Cited by W. Robertson Nicoll, <u>The Incarnate Saviour</u> (Edinburgh, T and T Clark, 1899) p. 10.

THE FLOODTIDE OF WRATH

PSALM 69:1

On April 10, 1912 the Titanic set out to sea. She was billed as "the unsinkable ship," some 66,000 tons of mechanics and magnificence. Five days later she sank through countless fathoms of water to the bottom of the sea. What happened? She struck an iceberg, and it tore a 300-foot gash in her side. The waters outside the ship came surging in—and the unsinkable ship was sunk.

Two thousand years ago, on a clear and starry night, in a remote Judean town, God launched a mighty Vessel on the seas of time, an unsinkable ship indeed, engineered in eternity, to plans and blueprints drawn up before ever time began. The vessel itself was fashioned by the Holy Ghost in a virgin's womb. It was launched with scarcely a ripple to disturb mankind. There, in the small village of Bethlehem, the Son of God became the Son of Man.

Seas of sin surged all around Him even as He opened His eyes. A monster of a man sat on the throne that was rightfully His, a man who tried to murder Him. He was too late, the ship had already gone.

He grew up in an ordinary home. His brothers and sisters had sin natures just like everyone else. He, however, in stark and staring contrast, lived a sinless life. There was no crack, no flaw to be found in Him. As man He was innocent and beyond reproof; as God He was holy, and absolutely without any taint of sin.

He plowed through the seas of time until He came to Calvary and there the iceberg struck, and the seas of sin surged into His soul. He sank swiftly. Sin (not His, but ours, for He Himself was sinless) was DESTROYING HIM. "Save Me, O God," He said, "for the waters are come in unto my soul." He who for countless ages had known sin, as an omniscient Observer, now knew sin by becoming sin. "Save me!" He cried. He was answered by total silence. There was no Savior provided for Him. There was no Savior possible for Him if we were to be saved from sin.

Then, too, He felt that sin was DEFILING HIM. "Save me, O God . . . I sink in deep mire . . ." It was as though all the filthiness and all the impu-

16

rity of the human race had been gathered together in one vast, stinking quagmire; and He was being plunged beneath its loathsome ooze. The unbelievable horror of it had caused Him to sweat blood in Gethsemane and caused Him to cry in anguish at Golgotha.

But then, as though all that were not enough, He felt that sin was DROWN-ING HIM: "Save me, O God . . . I am come into deep waters where the floods overflow me." Down, down He went; and all God's billows rolled over Him. Noah, in his day, had his ark; but Jesus was left to sink, abandoned by man and by God. Jonah cried from "the belly of hell" and was heard. Jesus cried in vain.

"Save me!" He cried. No answer came. Instead, the tempest's voice was heard. The wind shrieked across a sunless sea, and the angry waves of wrath built themselves into marching mountains. He who once had stilled the storm with a word; who once had walked upon the angry deep, now sank beneath the waves, dragged down by the inconceivable weight of a whole world's sin.

And that seemed to be the end of it. He died and was taken down from the cross and put in a tomb. For three days and three nights the world continued to spin in space—a graveyard for His lifeless form. Then:

> "Up from the grave He arose,
> With a mighty triumph o'er His foes;
> He arose a victor from the dark domain
> And He lives forever with His saints to reign.
> He arose! He arose! Hallelujah, Christ arose."

"THEY THAT SEE ME"

PSALM 22:7

Abandoned by God (Ps 22:1-6). Abhorred by men (7-10). Who could this be? Friendless, forsaken, betrayed by all? The answer is even more terrible than the question—God's own Son, the uncreated, self-existing, second Person of the Godhead, manifest in flesh. Surely, as we stand on the threshold of this awesome twenty-second psalm, we should remove the shoes from off our feet, for the place whereon we stand is holy ground. He who hung there on that cross was the One who hung the stars. Those iron

bolts of Rome could have become thunderbolts in His hands to annihilate
His foes. Instead we see Him exposed to The Contempt Of Men (7-10).

They laughed Him to scorn. They made faces at Him and nodded their
heads at Him. They said: "He trusted in the Lord to deliver Him." The
word used here for trusted occurs no where else—"Roll it on Jehovah,"
they said, "Roll it on Him." They jeered thus at the very time when it
seemed that even God had let Him down.

Then, too, He was exposed to <u>The Cruelty Of Men</u> (11-17).

They surrounded Him, the psalmist said, like strong bulls of Bashan,
like roaring lions, like wild dogs. The words paint a picture of His enemies
circling the cross like so many wild beasts. Now one darts in with a taunt,
now another pushes close with a wisecrack, then another with a curse.
Moreover, He was exposed to <u>The Callousness Of Men</u> (18).

Now it was the turn of the soldiers. They soon tired of mocking jests
and the bitter taunts and they simply turned their backs on Him. What
cared they for His suffering? They had crucified people often enough
before. This was just another execution. They nailed Him to the cross,
dropped it into its socket with nerve-tearing thud, then turned away to
seize upon His legacy, His robe. They made short work of dividing up His
garments then they gathered around to gamble for His robe, a raiment
angels would have worn with pride.

Had Mark Anthony been there, as he had been years ago at the funeral
of Julius Caesar, he would have drawn special attention to that robe, as he
did to murdered Caesar's robe when he held up Caesar's robe for all the
world to see. Shakespeare records his words:[1]

> *"Friends," he said, "Romans, Countrymen,*
> *If you have tears, prepare to shed them now,*
> *You all do know this mantle; I remember*
> *The first time ever Caesar put it on . . .*
> *Look, in this place ran Cassius' dagger through,*
> *See what a rent the envious Cascar made . . .*
> *Great Caesar fell.*
> *Oh what a fall was there. . . ."*

Did Peter, we wonder, take that robe, not in substance but in imagery,
at Pentecost and spread it out, blood stained, before the people as he

charged them with the murder of the Son of God? Perhaps not! But just the same he had words more eloquent, more terrible than any that Shakespeare put into the mouth of Anthony. "Him ye have taken" he declared, "and have crucified and slain. . . ."

For all their contempt, all their cruelty, all their callousness came home to roost at Pentecost. A Spirit-emboldened Peter preached to the suddenly awakened conscience of the Jews.

How wonderful that, by then, the contempt, the cruelty and the callousness of men was to be answered not just in conviction and condemnation but with the infinite compassion of God. The cross was no longer just a gallows. It had become an instrument of grace.

---

¹William Shakespeare, <u>Julius Caesar</u>, Act III, Scene II.

SUCH AN HIGH PRIEST
HEBREWS 8:1

When an Old Testament sinner came to the altar with his offering, it was up to the priest to guide him through the various rituals specified for the particular kind of offering being brought.

It might be a sin offering, for instance. The sinner would be required to lay his hand upon the sacrifice. Then he must take the proffered knife and personally slay the lamb. The priest would then dismember it and examine it. If it passed the test he would place it on the fire and the sinner would see it burned to ashes in his stead. He would go away feeling much better about his sin.

Before long, however, he might have doubts. He would go back to the priest. "Do you know," he might say, "I really don't feel any different than I did before? Are you sure that the blood of that lamb really took away my sin?" The priest would say, "I suppose so. At least, the Law prescribes such and such a sacrifice for such and such a sin. I cannot tell you any more than that." It was all very unsatisfactory. The New Testament underlines the point. The book of Hebrews says: "It is not possible for the blood of bulls and goats to take away sins" (10:4). As the hymn writer says:

> *"Not all the blood of beasts*
> *On Jewish altars slain,*
> *Could give the guilty conscience peace*
> *Nor wash away one stain."*

Not very satisfactory one would say.

Some years ago I was in Vichy in France. It is a busy spa health resort to which people come from all over the world to take the cure. Brooding over the town is the Roman Catholic Church of Our Lady of Healing where a black statue of Mary dominates all. It was the dome, however, which most impressed me. High up in the dome is a picture. In that picture Christ is in the shadows, and Mary fills the foreground. The picture is so painted that Mary's robe lights up when the sun shines on it. She stands triumphant, trampling a writhing serpent. On the base of the dome are two quotations. One reads: "God so loved the world He gave His only Son", (a quotation from John 3:16). The other one, executed in letters which dwarf the Bible text, gives a quotation from Saint Bernard: "It is God's will that we obtain all things through Mary!" That painting struck me forcibly with the realization that the Virgin Mary is Rome's great mediator, not Christ.

A moment's thought, however, shows the fallacy of that. All over the world, at any given moment, thousands of devout Catholics are praying to Mary. She is bombarded with countless prayers in thousands of tongues. To hear them all, she would need to be <u>omnipresent</u>. To unravel them all, and be cognizant of them all, she would need to be <u>omniscient</u>. To respond to them all, she would need to be <u>omnipotent</u>. "If you want anything," says Rome, "then go to Mary." But Mary is not God. She has none of the attributes of deity. So, why pray to Mary? Not very satisfactory we might well say.

We need not a woman, however renowned and revered, nor a fallible priest, whether of Rome or anywhere else. We need a priest, "able to save to the uttermost" those that "come unto God by Him . . . a priest who ever liveth to make intercession" (Heb. 7:25).

Thankfully we have "such an High Priest." He is our Mediator with the Father (1 Tim. 2:5). He is all we need. He is a <u>powerful</u> High Priest, for in the tradition of Melchizedek (Gen. 14:18-20; Heb. 7:10) He is both

Priest and King. He is a permanent High Priest for He is alive for evermore and has the keys of death and Hades (Rev 1:18). He is a perfect High Priest free from all sin, and able to deal with ours (Heb 9:7, 11-14). And He is a patient High Priest "touched with the feeling of our infirmities" (Heb 4:15), being both God and Man and therefore able to make intercession for us. Very satisfactory indeed!

AN ALL-POWERFUL HIGH PRIEST
HEBREWS 7:1-17

The Lord Jesus is introduced to us as "a high priest after the order of Melchizedek." For, like the Old Testament Melchizedek, He is both a priest and a king—something no priest of Aaron's line could ever be.

Hebrews 7:1-2 puts the emphasis on the kingly aspect of the Melchizedek priesthood: "For this Melchizedek," says the Holy Spirit, "was king of Salem, priest of the most high God. . . being by interpretation king of righteousness, after that also king of Salem, which is king of peace." The title is repeated four times—King! King! King! King!

We read of Abraham's encounter with Priest-King Melchizedek in Genesis 14. Abraham had just won a military victory over a vastly superior force—a coalition of all-victorious kings of the East who, having devastated the Sodomites and their allies, were returning home laden with the spoils of war and with many captives. Abraham's nephew, Lot, and his family, were among those captives. With a mere handful of men Abraham launched a night attack, surprised the invaders, put them to flight and recovered the spoil and the captives.

He had suddenly become the most powerful man in Canaan. He could have dictated whatever terms he liked to the neighboring chieftains. Instead, he turned his back on it all realizing he was a pilgrim, and a stranger on earth. The surrounding chieftains, by contrast, called him "a prince and a great man."

It was then that Abraham met Melchizedek, one who was able to bestow upon the pilgrim patriarch the true riches of righteousness and peace. The Canaanite chieftains in the area did not seem to know the value of a man like Melchizedek. Abraham did. Melchizedek was an Old Testament type of Christ, a man in touch with God and Abraham instantly recognized his worth. He came and sat at this man's feet in deep humility. Far from triumph going to Abraham's head, it brought him to Melchizedek's feet. Nowhere does Abraham's spiritual stature show better than here.

The triumph gives way to the table, for Abraham at once took his place as a guest at Melchizedek's table. Bread and wine were on that table—symbols of the Lord's passion. The bread and the wine pointed forward to the coming One whose body would be broken and whose blood would be shed.

Then came the title for, at the table of Melchizedek, Abraham learned a new name for God. He is "the most High God, Possessor of heaven and earth." All the riches of earth and all the resources of heaven, were in His hand. No wonder Abraham could afford to take a carefree attitude toward material things. The "God Most High" was his God.

Now comes the test. The King of Sodom came with his offer of a deal. "You take the spoils," he said, "and I'll take the souls." Abraham did not even have to think. He wanted nothing to do with Sodom, its goods or its king. Abraham loathed Sodom and all it stood for. The Possessor of heaven and earth was his God. What need had he of spoils of war or Sodom's gold? "I'll not have you say that you made Abraham rich," he said to Sodom's king. This spiritual victory stemmed from Abraham's recognition of Melchizedek as his own King-Priest.

We, today, are better off than Abraham by far for, Melchizedek, when all is said and done, was only a type of Christ. We have Christ Himself, a powerful Priest enthroned in heaven as God Most High and the Possessor of heaven and earth. What more could we want than that?

THE EMMAUS ROAD
LUKE 24:1-33

There they go, two of the Lord's disciples and, it might well be, man and wife, at that. Their backs are towards Jerusalem, the city which historically had stoned the prophets and martyred God's ministers and which, but lately had murdered its Messiah. Their faces are towards the village of Emmaus.

It was a seven-mile hike into the country. These sad disciples walked with feet of lead, as heavy as their heavy hearts. And, of course, they talked together. Enough things had happened in Jerusalem over the past few days to keep them talking for a very long time. The wonder-working Jesus had come riding into the city, hailed by the people as the very Messiah Himself. The religious establishment, however determined to put Him to death, had bought Judas, browbeaten Pilate and manipulated the mob. They had hounded wonder-working Jesus of Nazareth to the cross and to His death. Now, three days later, it was evidently all over and they were going home talking about these things as they followed the mountain road.

Then Jesus came up alongside, but they did not know it was He. They thought He was just a fellow traveler. We get three glimpses of these disciples on that never to be forgotten Emmas road.

How Mistaken They Were. This stranger, who had joined them, seemed to them to be astoundingly ignorant of the tremendous events which had stirred the whole country for weeks. "Art thou only a stranger in Jerusalem and hast not known the things which are come to pass there in these days?" they said.

What a question! He was no stranger in Jerusalem. He had watched over its history for 2000 years. Indeed, if the truth were told, it was His city. As for the recent events which had taken place there, well He knew more about those things than they did because they had all happened to Him! He had scars on his back and wounds in his hands and feet and side to prove it. These two Emmaus disciples walked six or seven miles with Jesus and didn't know it was He Himself who talked to them. How often have we failed to recognize Him too? We note, too, How Miserable They Were. It was patently obviously to Jesus that these disciples were discouraged, totally demoralized and completely downcast. They spilled it all out, the sad story of their crucified hopes. "We trusted that it had been He which should have redeemed Israel, "they said.

Well! Whatever had He been doing on the cross if He hadn't been providing redemption for Israel—and for all mankind? Redemption has to do with paying a price for something of great value, often pawned for little more than a song. And what a price He had paid! The price of our redemption was His own most precious blood poured out in as agony on the cross. They did not understand that. No wonder misery had been their shadow on that long walk to Emmaus.

Finally, How Moved They Were. Then the stranger began to talk. He gave them a Bible survey, reviewing for them all that the prophets had written and showing them in all the scriptures the things concerning Himself. He talked to them about the covering God had provided for fallen, naked Adam and Eve. He talked about Noah and his ark, about Joseph, about the Passover and the offerings, about Isaiah 53, and Psalm 22 and Psalm 69.

Their hearts burned. And it was this inspired exegesis of the Bible that did it! Then suddenly the journey was over. They were home! They asked Him in and showed Him to His place at the table. It seemed only natural to ask Him to give thanks for the food, so He blessed and broke the bread. And they saw His hands! And He was gone! They hurried back to Jerusalem with songs. He was alive! And they arrived in the upper room just in time to see Him again!

He is still at it! Opening unto us the scriptures, making our hearts burn within us, giving us glimpses of Himself. Blessed be His name!

THE GRACE OF OUR LORD JESUS CHRIST
2 CORINTHIANS 8:9

Paul takes it for granted that we know at least something of the grace of the Lord Jesus Christ. Just the same, he challenges us to know more. He sets before us two things—two things calculated to stir us to the depth of our being. First, he gives us a glimpse of <u>Superlative Grace</u>. "Ye know the grace of our Lord Jesus Christ that, though He was rich, yet for your sakes He became poor."

We know that He was rich, but we have no idea how rich He really was. We sometimes sing:

"My Savior is rich in houses and land
He holdeth the wealth of the world in His hand."

But that is only a small part of it. In the land from whence He came, they pave their streets with gold. The towering walls of His great city are made of jasper, its gates of solid pearl and its twelve foundations are ablaze with priceless gems. Before He came down here, He sat in splendor on a great white throne while shining seraphim hung upon His words and rushed to do His will. All his ministers were a flame of fire. All the vast galactic empires of the stars belonged to Him. Had He so desired He could have created galaxies of gold.

So then, we know that He was rich, but we cannot tell how rich He was. Only one or two of Adam's race have ever been to <u>His</u> land and returned to tell the tale. Even then they have difficulty telling what they saw. Paul was there and declared that what he saw was untranslatable. John was there and he resorts to symbolic language when telling us what that place is like. So, then, we know that He was rich. We do not know how rich He was.

We know, too, that for our sakes, He became poor but, again, we do not know how poor He was. He was born in a borrowed barn. When He wanted to teach the crowding multitudes, He had to borrow Simon Peter's boat to be His stage. To feed the hungry multitudes, He had to borrow a little lad's lunch. To ride through Jerusalem in triumph, to fulfill an ancient prophesy, He had to borrow a donkey from a friend. To keep His last Passover, He had to borrow someone's upper room. He died upon another man's cross and was buried in a borrowed tomb. Foxes had their holes, and birds of the air had their nests but He had nowhere to lay His head.

Then, too, we have <u>Superlative Gain</u>. "Why," we ask. "Why did He who was so superlatively rich become so startlingly poor? "That ye," says Paul, "through His poverty might be made rich." First He canceled all our debt. We are the ten thousand talent debtors of whom Jesus spoke. We are the bankrupts with nothing to pay. He took all our debt, ours and ten thousand times ten thousand other debts beside, took it to Calvary and beggared Himself to cancel it all.

But more! He has made us rich. He has made us Sons of God and joint-heirs with Himself. He has seated us with Himself in the heavenlies in a realm beyond the sky and He has endowed us with all the riches of His grace. Now He is building for us mansions in glory and promised us that where He is there we shall be also.

Such is "the grace of our Lord Jesus Christ. "Selah!" as David would say, "What do you think of that?"

THE WEDDING AT CANA
JOHN 2:1-11

It is a memorable fact that the Lord's first public miracle was performed at a wedding and His last public miracle was performed at a funeral. Thus we seem Him Master of every situation—at life's <u>gladdest</u> hour and at life's <u>saddest hour</u>.

There are two things we might observe about the wedding at Cana. First there is <u>The Wedding Guest</u>. It says something for the bride and groom that they invited Jesus and His disciples to their wedding. How thankful they must have been when the crisis arose, that they had included Him when they thought of their marriage feast. And He came! Of course, He did, as He comes to every wedding to which He is called. It was some ninety miles from where He was to Cana where they were, but He came. And He came to bless.

John tells us nothing about the ceremony, nothing about the bride and groom, nothing about the other guests, save for Mary. From the prominence of Mary, and the way she spoke to the servants, this may have been the wedding of one of her nephews or nieces, or even, perhaps, that of one of her children. Tradition gives the names of Esther and Thamar to the sisters of Jesus. His brothers were James, Joses, Simon and Judas (Matt. 13:55). Perhaps it was one of these who was getting married that day. Whoever the bride and groom were, they knew Jesus and He was their specially invited wedding guest.

Then there was <u>The Wedding Gift</u>. No doubt the couple received many wedding gifts that day; Jesus kept His until last. So, the wedding took place and the banquet began. Then tragedy struck. Someone whispered to Mary—"We've run out of wine." In those days, and to this day in eastern lands, lavish hospitality was a sacred duty. Gloom, mortification, bitter, indelible disgrace was about to ruin everything. Total calamity loomed.

"They have no wine!" As F. W. Boreham says somewhere, in one of his books, life always breaks down on the side of its exhilaration's, its excitements, its joys. Mary passed on the sad news to Jesus. He gently disengaged Himself from anything which might have suggested He acted on her request or wish. He knew too well how far some would go in the coming ages to promote her instead of Him.

Then He went to work, as He always does, quietly, competently, gloriously. There was plenty of water, even if there was no wine! He would simply turn the one into the other.

It is a long, slow process to turn water into wine. A vine must be planted. Water and nourishment must be drawn up from its roots to its branches. It must produce flowers. Insects must come and pollinate the plant. Little clusters of emerging grapes must appear. They must grow as rain and sunshine do their work. When ripe, the grapes must be picked and crushed. The flowing juice must be put in vats. It must ferment, and it must turn into wine. Jesus simply telescoped the whole process into a miracle. As someone has said:

> *"The simple water, touched by grace divine*
> *Owned its Creator, and blushed into wine."*

It was not hard for Him. After all—is He not <u>the</u> Vine (John 15:1)? No doubt the bride and groom never stopped thanking their special <u>wedding guest</u> for His special <u>wedding gift</u>.

AT THE CROSS
LUKE 23:33-49

The world was at the cross. There were Jews present in Jerusalem from all parts of Palestine and from the remotest regions of the Diaspora. The titles, nailed to the cross of Jesus, were written in Greek and Latin and Hebrew, the three world languages of the day—Greek, the language of reason; Latin, the language of rule; Hebrew, the language of religion. Moreover, it was Passover time, and the normal population would be increased many times over by visitors from abroad. The world was at the cross—drawn to Canaan by the season and drawn to Calvary by the Savior, He Who said: "And I, if I be lifted up will draw all men unto me." Luke tells us of some who were there.

First, The Romans Were There. The Romans represented the vast, lost Gentile world. Their empire was full of pagans. They picture "the untold millions still untold," the multiplied millions of mankind without God, without Christ and without hope. The Romans were there with their gift for government, with their military might, with all their pomp and power, with their engineering, technology and science. They were able to conquer the world, but unable to conquer themselves. Practical, powerful and pagan. Calvary drew the likes of them.

Then, too, The Robbers Were There. The robbers represented the criminal class, those who defied the law, men who were guilty of open sins, brigands, insurrectionists, murderers and the like. They had been caught red-handed in the crimes. They had been condemned. They were now paying the price of their sin. The robbers were there, hurling insults in the face of God by reviling His Son.

And The Rabble Was There, the thoughtless, fickle mob. Jesus had healed their sick and raised their dead. He had fed their hungry multitudes, cast out tormenting demons who possessed them. He had made their lame to walk, their blind to see, their dumb to speak, their deaf to hear. They repaid Him by shouting for His death and by clamoring for an insurrectionist and murderer Barabbas by name. Now they were at Calvary to mock and jeer.

Most tragic of all, The Rabbis Were There—the rabbis with half the Bible memorized and the other half ignored. The rabbis who had so tin-

28

kered with the Holy Scriptures that they had now virtually buried the Bible beneath vast mountains of oral tradition. The rabbis were there to make quite sure that Jesus was dead and then go home to religiously keep the Sabbath and the Passover and imagine they had done God a favor. They were there mocking the Lord of Glory because He had saved others but could not save Himself.

So people came to Calvary, and the cross exposed them all. To the Jews, that cross was a scandal and a libel to suggest that the Messiah of Israel could die on a Roman tree under the curse of God. To the Greeks the cross made no sense. To them it was the height of folly to preach "Christ and Him crucified." To the Romans, the cross of Christ was just another jibbot. They would scoff at a King of the Jews nailed to a cross. Ah, but unto us who are saved by the blood that was shed on that cross, the cross is both the power of God and the wisdom of God. It is God's answer to man's sin. Our reaction to the preaching of the cross reveals our state of soul (1 Cor. 1:18-25).

A PERFECT HIGH PRIEST
HEBREWS 7:26

There are three things about our High Priest which enables Him to meet all our needs. First, He Is Holy. Picture the camp of Israel. The wilderness wanderings have brought the people to the frontiers of Moab. Down from the hills comes a Moabite, a man under a curse (Deut. 23:3). He has seen the Hebrew tribes spread out before him in perfect order. He has seen the fiery, cloudy pillar overshadowing the camp. He may even have heard of the eloquent prophecies of Balaam regarding Moab and Israel (Num. 22-24; 31:16) He is filled with curiosity. He approaches the door of the tabernacle, and there he is stopped. But he is full of questions.

The man at the gate explains to the Moabite that of all days for him to come, he happens to have come on the Day of Atonement. The High Priest, yonder in the gorgeous robes, will soon enter into the holy of holies itself. He will take the blood of a goat with him to sprinkle on the mercy seat.

The man from Moab asks a question: "And what about that bullock over there?" He is told: "The goat is to atone for the sins of everyone but the bullock is for the sins of the high priest! Before he can confess the sins of the people, he must first confess his own. Indeed, his sins are much worse, in the sight of God, than anyone else's. That's why he needs a bullock while a goat will do for everyone else.

There is something disappointing about that. We want a priest who is holy. The nation of Israel, in some 1500 years never had such a high priest. But that is exactly what we have in Jesus—a holy high Priest.

Then, too, our high priest has something else we need in a priest. He Is Human. As the conversation between the Moabite and the man at the gate continues, someone barges in. "Of course, we need a holy priest," he says, "but there is something very cold, to my mind, about goodness in the abstract. I find the thought of an absolutely sinless high priest formidable. I want someone a little more human—someone who knows from experience what it is like to be full of infirmities. I don't want a sinful high priest, but I certainly want a sympathetic one—someone who knows what it is liked to be tempted and tried. Thank God for Jesus! He is thoroughly human. He understands us wonderfully well.

Finally, He Is Helpful. Someone else speaks up, adding to the conversation: "I want someone who can be helpful," he says. "Why even the high priest of Israel can only stay in the holy of holies long enough to sprinkle the blood. He certainly cannot stay in there. He cannot go in there whenever he likes. And, in any case, this tabernacle is only a temporary affair. None of this is very helpful to me."

"I want Someone bigger than Moses, Someone better than Aaron and Someone beyond even Melchizedek. I want Someone who is man, but who is more than man. I want Someone who is sinless but who is also sympathetic—Someone who not only knows me but who loves me. I want Someone who can deal with my sins and who can enter the holy of holies in heaven on my behalf. I need Someone who can invite me to enter into the holy of holies. I need Someone who can satisfy God and silence Satan and still my conscience and make me good."

Well, thank God, we have such an high priest. His name is Jesus. God says, "For such an high priest became us, who is holy, harmless, undefiled, separate from sinners, made higher than the heavens." Thank God for Him.

The Unforgetable Thrill
Revelation 5

John, caught up to heaven saw an unforgettable <u>Throng</u>! He also saw an unforgettable <u>Throne</u>! Now he experiences an unforgettable <u>Thrill</u>. The Lamb of God is about to be placed in the spotlight of eternity, now and forever more.

First, the <u>Challenge of God Is Proclaimed Throughout The Universe</u>.

John saw a scroll in the hand of Him that sat upon the throne. It was the title deed of Earth. "Who is worthy to take the scroll?" That was the question. "Who is fit to govern the globe?" No one! That was the answer. The question was not, "Who is willing?" for, in that case, there would have been a stampede, but "Who is worthy." A deep silence stole across the universe. Then that silence was shattered by a sob. "I wept much," said John. He wept for the shame of it, that no man of Adam's ruined race was good enough or great enough to take those title deeds and rule the world.

Then the <u>Christ of God Is Presented Throughout The Universe</u>. One of the elders could stand it no longer. Tears enough are known on earth, but tears in heaven? "Weep not," the elder said, "behold the Lion of the tribe of Judah has prevailed to take the scroll." John turned to see this Lion. Instead He saw the <u>Lamb</u>! Right there! Where he had been looking all along! Right there in the midst of the elders, the cherubim and the throne, right where He belonged "in the midst." John had been so taken up with the sights and sounds of heaven he missed the Lamb.

Jesus is called the Lamb only twice in the Old Testament, only twice in the Gospels, only once in the book of Acts and only once in the epistles—but no less than twenty-eight times in the book of Revelation.

Moreover, the word for "Lamb," here, literally means "a <u>Little Lamb</u>." In the book of Revelation, Satan appears as a great red dragon and the Antichrist as a wild beast with seven heads and ten horns. They mobilize the massed might of the world against God and His own. All God needs in response is a little Lamb! But this is no ordinary Lamb. This Lamb has seven horns suggesting His (omnipotence) and seven eyes symbolizing His (omniscience). It is the Lamb of Calvary! He comes and takes the scroll. For He, while truly "God over all blessed for evermore," is yet a Son, a child of Adam's race. Moreover He is a sinless One. He is fit to rule the world. From now on all judgment is delivered to the Son.

Now the Choice Of God Is Praised. All heaven breaks into the Hallelujah Chorus! And all hell is forced to bring to Him its own answering tribute of praise. The Lamb is praised first at the focal center of things. "They sang a new song" we read, right there in Glory. "Thou art worthy for Thou wast slain," they say. As the old hymn puts it:

> *"When in yonder glory*
> *I sing the new, new song;*
> *'Twill be the old, old story*
> *hat I have loved so long."*

Ten thousand times ten thousand voices will be raised in heaven and the universe will echo back the sounds of praise.

Then, too, the Lamb will be praised at the furthest circumference of things. Fallen angels and demons, principalities, powers, rulers of this world's darkness and wicked spirits in high places along with fallen, God-hating men, even Satan himself—all will be forced to join the chorus— "Blessing, honor, glory, power be unto Him that sitteth upon the throne, and unto the Lamb for ever and ever."

Blessed be God our God!

JOHN AND THE RESURRECTION
JOHN 1:1-10

John took his pen in hand to write his gospel towards the end of the first century. The Church was under attack—persecution from without, perversion from within. Apostasy was entrenched in high places. The third generation was now in charge, and truth was put up for sale.

In the first generation of a movement, conviction rules. Truth, dearly bought, is defended to the death. In the second generation, conviction degenerates into belief. People, raised in the great truths they have been taught, believe them and will argue for them; but the passion and the power has gone. In the third generation, belief becomes <u>opinion</u>; and opinions can be easily changed. John wrote for this perilous third generation which was busy selling its birthright for a mess of this world's pottage. He took his readers back to the beginning.

It was all as fresh and as vivid in his mind as though it were but yesterday. His thoughts flew back to the wonderful years he had spent in the company of Jesus. He would write about them. The skeptics, liberals, and gnostics could be silenced by John in three words: "I was there!" He would take that careless third generation back to where it all began. John, of course, realized that the world itself could not contain the books which he could have written about Jesus. So he concentrated on a few special <u>signs</u> and <u>sayings</u> of Jesus. And, of course, he had some important things to say about the resurrection, the cornerstone of our faith.

So far as John was concerned, his recollection of all the wonderful happenings of the resurrection day began with a woman. Her love for Jesus (living or dead) drove her from her bed before the break of day. She must have been a brave woman. She was not afraid of the dark, nor of the guard, nor of being alone in a cemetery. Perfect love had cast out all her fear. But there was no guard! The stone was rolled away! The tomb was empty! She fled on winged feet to tell John.

So it was, still early in the morning, John and Peter came to see for themselves. And this is what John saw—graveclothes. They spoke volumes to him.

When burying their dead, the Jews took linen cloths and made bandages of them, tearing them into long strips—fine linen for the rich, old rags for the poor. Then they took large quantities of myrrh and aloes. They saturated the linen strips with liquid spices and wound them round and round the body. As they dried these linen strips hardened and formed a rigid casing around the body.

John saw the bandages lying in the tomb stiff, like a tube. He saw the napkin, folded and lying apart. He could see the hole in the mummy wrapping where the body once had been. There was a space between the head-shaped napkin and the tube-shaped body-clothes, where the neck should have been. But there was nothing there but empty space. The turban-shaped head napkin was empty. The tubular-shaped body wrappings, stark and stiff like a canister, were empty. There could be only one explanation.

Christ had risen right through the graveclothes. He was gone! The grave-clothes remained. John was convinced. The Lord was risen indeed.

JESUS AND HIS BIBLE
ISAIAH 53:1

The first glimpse we get of Jesus, between His birth and His baptism, He was in the midst—His rightful place, right at the heart of things. This time He was in the midst of the doctors, the famous rabbis to whose schools rich men sent their sons. He was there, listening to them and asking them questions. He made no attempt to teach them, for at the age of twelve, that would have been considered presumptuous. But a wise person knows how to direct and develop peoples' thoughts by asking them appropriate and challenging questions.

Doubtless these rabbis were wrapped up in the so-called "oral law." According to the rabbis this oral law was given by Moses to supplement the written Law. The custodians of this fictitious "oral law" kept adding to it. It did not contain divine truth in all its pristine purity, but the teachings and the traditions of men. By the time of the Middle Ages, it had grown to the size of the Encyclopedia Britannica and was carried in the capacious minds and memories of a handful of prodigies. Already in Jesus' day, this so-called oral law was given precedence over the written word of God and was on the way to becoming what we now call the Talmud. It was already replacing the Torah as the final authority in the matters of faith and morals.

So, we can well imagine what kind of questions Jesus posed to these rabbis—"What think ye of Christ, whose Son is He?" "Of whom does Isaiah 53 speak, of the prophet or of some other man?" "If David, in the Spirit, in Psalm 110 called the Messiah "Lord," how is He then his son?"

By the time He was thirty years of age, Jesus knew His Bible in Hebrew and Greek as no man before or since. No doubt He had memorized it and, along with it, all the teachings and traditions which fenced it in.

Isaiah 53 begins with the Lord and His Bible. The prophet begins with a sigh: "Who hath believed our report?" he asks. Practically nobody! For, as Jesus once declared, "A prophet is not without honor except in His own country and among His own people."

By the time Isaiah wrote chapter 53 of his book he was getting used to being ignored. For instance; he had foretold the coming Assyrian invasion and had been ignored. His prophecies had been fulfilled, however, for where once the great cities of Israel had stood, now the lion roared and the jackal roamed. He warned next of the coming Babylonian invasion—and was ignored. Now, in this matchless chapter, he told of a coming, suffering Messiah. Again, he was ignored.

Well, there was one Man Who read Isaiah 53 with unswerving belief—Jesus! "Who hath believed our report?" cried Isaiah. Jesus believed it! He believed every word of it. To Him every word was inerrant, inspired and God-breathed. And the whole chapter speaks of Him.

We can picture the Lord Jesus soaking up the scriptures at His mother's knee and then at the feet of the local rabbi in the Nazareth synagogue. Soon He was to be seen studying the scriptures on His own. He would ponder its passages even as He pounded nails into a board in the workshop at Nazareth. He based His whole life on God's Word. When He came to live in this world He could say: "Lo I come, in the volume of the book it is written of Me, to do Thy will O My God" (Ps. 40:7; Heb. 10:7). Every move He made was in keeping with that word.

"Yes! Isaiah," He would say, pausing at each verse, each phrase, each clause of Isaiah 53, "I believe that. That is written of me. That's me! I am going to experience that, suffer that, fulfill that. Who believes you? I do. And it is going to cost me my life."

THE LORD AND HIS BOYHOOD
ISAIAH 53:2

There never was a boy like Jesus. Isaiah tells us two things about the boyhood of our Lord. First, He tells us How Holy He Was. He says: "He shall grow up before Him as a tender plant"—that has to do with his nature. "And as a root out of a dry ground." That has to do with His nurture. Both set Him apart from all other boys.

A tender plant! Over the years I have preached at Park of the Palms, a retirement center in Florida. At one time, the grounds were kept beautiful by a retired, professional gardener. Only, once, did I hear him address an audience. This is what he said:

"On a stormy night in winter I like to pull up my chair to the fire and get out my seed catalogues and plan my garden for the coming year. All plants featured in a seed catalog are described in one of three ways. They are either hardy, half-hardy, or tender. There are some very real differences, I can assure you, between these various categories.

"A hardy plant is one native to the area. It will take ready root because it feels at home. The soil, the climate, the weather are all congenial. A half-hardy plant is one which is not a native to the area, but it comes from a similar environment. The conditions are much the same so it quickly settles in as a native. But a tender plant—well that's a different story. It is an exotic plant. It comes from far away. It does not find the soil or the climate congenial. It will need special attention. It will have to be protected from the weather. It will have to be fed special nutrients. It is a tender plant."

"Our Lord Jesus was in this sin-cursed world as a tender plant. He came from far away. His nature was not like our nature. This world's sin-ridden social, secular and spiritual climate was foreign to Him. He was holy and harmless and undefiled and separate from sinners. He was a transplant from glory. He came out of eternity into time. As man, He was absolutely innocent; as God, He was absolutely holy. He was holy even as a boy. He was good, as God is good. He had no sin nature. "Satan cometh," He said, toward the end of His life, "Satan cometh and hath nothing in me." He was a tender plant, from another land, a land beyond the sky. He was a transplant from Glory. This sin-cursed world of ours was not His real home."

The prophet goes on to describe His nurture. By the time Jesus came down here the major pagan world religions had long since been founded and given a chance to show what mere religion can do. Little enough, if anything at all. The Lord found nothing in them. The great philosophers of Greece had come and gone and been given their chance to deal with the human condition. The Lord found nothing to nurture Him in them. Judaism had abandoned the Torah for the budding Talmud—the Mishna and the Midrash had already taken deep root. There was nothing to nurture

Him there—just the opinions and traditions of men. So he drove His roots deep into the Word of God. He was a root, indeed, out of a dry ground. He became the Blessed Man of Psalm 1, the Tree planted by the rivers of water, by the Spirit of God Himself. Isaiah tells us, moreover, <u>How Human He Was</u>. He was God-incarnate, burning with holiness but all His essential, innate glory was so veiled by His humanity that the prophet could add: "He hath no form nor comeliness; and when we shall see Him there is no beauty in Him that we should desire Him." All people saw was "the carpenter's son." They saw a man in a homespun robe, speaking the local dialect; and they dismissed Him as a Galilean peasant. They saw no beauty in Him at all. Indeed, the people of His native village tried to kill Him for telling them the truth. But God's eye was on Him. The angels were watching over Him. He was God's "Tender Plant," a transplant from another world, cultivated and protected by God while living in a hostile world.

A MAN OF SORROWS
ACQUAINTED WITH GRIEF
ISAIAH 53:3

"He is despised and rejected of men," says the prophet, "a man of sorrows and acquainted with grief!" The expression "man of sorrows" can be translated "man of pains." We would have found it easier to accept had Isaiah called Him "a man of war," or "a man of God," or "a man of might and miracle." But:

> *"Man of sorrows?' What a name,*
> *For the Son of God Who came*
> *Ruined sinners to reclaim!*
> *Hallelujah, what a Savior."*

Surely, if ever there was a man on earth who should have been exempt from suffering and pain, it was Jesus. But no! He was "a man of pain."

Not far from where I was born and brought up, there stands, on the bank of the river Wye, the stark but impressive ruins of an abbey. It has a history running back some seven or eight hundred years. It was founded and built by an agrarian order of monks and, like so many other abbeys in England, it grew to be rich and powerful. In time, indeed, the abbeys rivaled the very throne.

Henry VIII decided to put an end to all that. The vast holdings of the abbeys he gave to his favorites at court. The lead from the roofs of the abbeys was torn off, melted down and sold to enrich the king. The wind and the weather did the rest. All that remains of Tintern Abbey today is the walled skeleton of an impressive ruin. No one visiting the abbey would imagine, for a moment, that it was designed to be the ruin it now is. On the contrary, it was <u>designed</u> to be a magnificent building. It was never intended to be treated the way it was.

We live in a ruined world, a world of suffering, sorrow and death. But it was not designed that way. Tintern Abbey was designed to last almost forever; even its ruins bear witness to that. The ruined abbey presents us today with a mixture of order and chaos just as the world in which we live presents us with a mixture of order and chaos, of good and evil.

It was to deal with the ruin that Jesus came into the world. He did not come as a tourist to shake His head and mourn over the vast devastation done to His own handiwork. He came to deal with it. And that meant becoming involved. It meant becoming a man of sorrows, acquainted with grief. So Isaiah takes us to the cross.

Some time ago I read a book written by a man who went through the horrors of Auchwitz. He was a child when he was torn away from his home, loaded onto a boxcar and shipped across endless miles of misery to a place where torture and torment was the sum and substance of life. His mother and his little sister were murdered, and their bodies burned. A smudge of smoke was the last he saw of them. He survived. He was always hungry, always terrified, but he survived.

God died in this tormented prisoner's soul on the day he witnessed the hanging of a young boy. The commandment read the indictment, but all eyes were on the boy. He was hanged for stealing a potato and the inmates of the camp were forced to march past his gallows. The worst part of it was he was so light it took him a long time to die. The survivor collapsed into ruins himself that day. He heard someone in the ranks say, "Where is God now?" He said to himself, "God is dead." He added, "That night the soup tasted of corpses."

But God was not dead, is not dead. The answer to the bitter question, "Where is God now?", is simple. He is in the same place He was when His Son was hanged. For Jesus came to get involved. He became a man of sorrows, acquainted with grief. The answer to the problem of suffering, pain and death in the world is bound up with the suffering, pain and death of Jesus. And with His glorious resurrection, ascension and certain return.

HE AND ME

ISAIAH 53:4-6

He and me! Not very good grammar, perhaps, but very good gospel. Let us read what the prophet says, putting the emphasis on ourselves:

"Surely He hath borne OUR grief's, and carried OUR sorrows, He was wounded for OUR transgressions, He was bruised for OUR iniquities: the chastisement of OUR peace was upon Him, and by His stripes WE are healed. WE have turned everyone to his own way, and the Lord hath laid on Him the iniquity of US all. Amazing! All for us.

But the statement becomes all the more amazing when we turn it around and put all the emphasis on Him:

"Surely HE hath bourne our grief's and carried our sorrows. HE was wounded for our transgressions. HE was bruised for our iniquities: the chastisement of our peace was upon HIM, and by HIS stripes we are healed. We have turned everyone to his own way, and the Lord hath laid on HIM the iniquity of us all. As the hymn says:

> *"And when I think that God His SON not sparing*
> *Sent HIM to die I scarce can take it in.*
> *That on the cross, my burden gladly bearing*
> *HE bled and died to take away my sin."*

"He was wounded for our transgressions," the prophet declares. There are five kinds of wounds we can suffer. There is a contused wound, one which results from a blow delivered by a blunt instrument. The Lord suffered that kind of a wound when they blindfolded Him, and some brute of a man drew back his fist and punched Him with all his force in the face.

There is a <u>laceration</u>, the kind of wound produced by a tearing instrument. The Lord suffered terrible lacerations when He was scourged. A Roman scourge was a fearful thing. The victim was bound to a post and beaten with a whip of numerous cords in which were embedded bits of iron or bone. The flesh was torn off the back and the organs exposed. It was not uncommon for a man to die under a scourging.

Then, too, there is a <u>penetrating</u> wound, a wound produced by a sharp-pointed instrument. The Lord suffered this kind of wound when He was crowned with thorns. The Jerusalem thorn has spikes four inches long. The mocking crown was pressed down upon His head producing a ring of wounds around His brow, deepened by subsequent blows to His head.

There is also a <u>perforating</u> wound, the kind of wound caused when the instrument pierces right through. The Lord suffered this wound when they pierced His hands and His feet.

Finally, there is an <u>incision</u> resulting from a cut produced by a sharp-edged instrument such as a knife or a sword. The last indignity done to the Lord's body was done with a Roman spear. That great gash in His side showed Him to be dead. So we sing:

> *"Wounded for me, wounded for me*
> *There on the cross He was wounded for me,*
> *Gone my transgressions and now I am free—*
> *All because Jesus was wounded for me . . ."*

When we sing that, we picture Him receiving all the wounds we can experience. Moreover, He carries the scars of those wounds to this very day, up there in Glory, to the wonder of the redeemed and all the hosts of heaven.

OUR LORD JESUS CHRIST
ROMANS 16:18

Two opposite considerations draw out our thoughts at the mention of this Name. In the first place, He is "our" Lord Jesus Christ. Evidently, the apostle is referring to the Christ of the Christian; but the context is quite different. The context has to do with those who embrace error, those who cannot correctly answer the Lord's own, piercing question: "What think ye of Christ, Whose Son is He?" For, in stark contrast with our Lord Jesus Christ, the Christ of the Christian, is their Lord Jesus Christ, the christ of the cults.

Our Lord Jesus Christ is Lord—He is the Master, the One who controls all things. He is the Creator and Sustainer of all things. He is the sovereign Lord of the universe, the One at whose name every knee will one day bow, the One to whom every tongue confess that He is Lord.

Our Lord Jesus Christ is beloved by all His own as Jesus—He is the Man. He became a man when He was born at Bethlehem, truly human in every sense of the word. He was born, He lived, He died, He rose again. Now He is enthroned on high and still He wears the scars of His sojourn on earth. Those scars are indelibly printed into His hands and feet and side. He knows what it is like to share our experiences as humans. He is sinless yet sympathetic, humble and holy, loving and lowly, patient and pure and kind. He is "Jesus!"

Our Lord Jesus is also the Christ—He is the Messiah, the "anointed" one, prophet, priest and king—a prophet to reveal, a priest to redeem and a prince to rule. Such is "our Lord Jesus Christ." "Our Lord Jesus Christ!" Such is His full and proper Name.

Now let us consider the Christ of the cults. There are the Liberals, for instance, who have a christ; but He is not our Lord Jesus Christ. Their christ was conceived out of wedlock, supposedly by some passing liaison between Mary and an unknown soldier—therefore subject to the terrible excommunication inflected on the illegitimate child by the Mosaic Law. Their christ performed no miracles, died as a martyr and rose again only in legend. Their christ is not our Lord Jesus Christ. Pity them!

The Jehovah's Witnesses have a christ, but he is not God, overall, blessed and forevermore. Their christ did not rise from the dead. The body of their christ dissolved in gases in the tomb. Nor is their christ the Second Person of the Godhead, a member of the Trinity, the Creator of the universe. Their christ is not our Lord Jesus Christ. Pity them!

The Mormons have a christ. But their christ was a polygamist, secretly married to Martha and Mary. Not, by any means is their christ "our Lord Jesus Christ."

The Catholics have a christ, but they make Him out of a piece of bread by reciting five Latin words over a wafer and turning it into the body, blood, soul and Divinity of Christ. They have a christ, but He is subordinate to Mary and is "conredemptrix" with her. He is not our Lord Jesus Christ.

"They that are such," says the Holy Spirit, "serve not our Lord Jesus Christ." Our Lord Jesus is God the Son. He entered into human life by being virgin born. He lived a sinless life, performed countless miracles and fulfilled scores of Old Testament prophecies. Our Lord Jesus Christ died an atoning death. He was buried and rose again the third day. He has ascended into heaven where He now sits at God's right hand as our Great High Priest, anticipating the day of His coming again. That is our Lord Jesus Christ.

Unto Us A Child Is born
Isaiah 9:6

"A child born!" says Isaiah, "a Son given!" Matthew and Luke tell us of the child that was born; John tells of the Son that was given. The child born! That points us to the Son of man. The Son given! That points us to the Son of God. The child born was the Babe of Bethlehem; the Son given was "the Lord from heaven." The Child born! That reminds us He was truly Man, the Son given tells us He was God, overall blessed forevermore. The Child born! That marks a beginning in time, the Son given is the ancient of days, from everlasting to everlasting. Jesus was both the child born and the Son given.

The prophet gives us a four-fold description of this glorious One born of the virgin Mary, conceived of the Holy Ghost.

He is "the wonderful counsellor." That is, there is <u>no problem He cannot solve</u>. There are some 27,000 psychiatrists in the United States alone. People go to them to pour out their anger, frustration, bitterness, hatred, fear, envy, and guilt—and the problems in our society multiply and grow more and more horrendous all the time. Obviously psychiatrists, psychologists, and social works, trained counsellors, do not have any real answers to the problems of people in general and society at large. But Jesus does! There is no problem He cannot solve. No one ever appealed to Him in vain. No one ever found Him at a loss. For "in Him are hid all the treasures of wisdom."

Then, too, He is "the mighty God." There is <u>no power He cannot subdue</u>. He is the "Creator of the rolling spheres, ineffably sublime." One Who can fling a hundred billion galaxies into space, or populate a drop of ditch water with countless microscopic germs, or pack enough power into an atom to incinerate a city can surely put down at will any power on earth or in heaven or in hell.

Moreover, there is <u>no period He does not span</u>. He is "the Father of Eternity." We go back, ever further back in time, and always He is there. Back we go to the moment of the "big bang" and on back beyond that moment. And there <u>He</u> is, about to launch countless stars and their satellites into vast orbits, at inconceivable velocities, to travel with mathematical precision on predictable paths! Always He is there—inescapable, gathering all time into the eternal present tense.

And, too, there is <u>no person He cannot save</u>. For the One who sits astride the centuries, who walks amid the galaxies, who has all wisdom and who dwells amid great certainties has nail prints in His hands. He is mighty to save: "Whosoever will may come," He says. That Child born, that Son given is our Savior and our Lord. And, blessed be God our God, He is our peace.

COME DOWN
NEHEMIAH 6:3

Up went the walls! Such was the drive, the determination and the discipline of Nehemiah that it took only fifty-two days to accomplish the task, less than two months. But not without opposition. One of the wiles of the foe was to try to lure Nehemiah away. We note The Proposal: "Come," said Sanballet and Geshem to the Jewish leader, "Come, let us meet together, in one of the villages" (6:2). The proposal would have meant a journey of at least twenty-five miles. "They thought to do me mischief," Nehemiah said. He saw right through their somewhat transparent plot.

We note also The Priority: "I am doing a great work," said Nehemiah, "so that I cannot come down: why should the work cease while I leave it and come down to you?" And that was that. So far as Nehemiah was concerned nothing mattered more than completing the repair of Jerusalem's walls.

It is important to have our priorities right. Nehemiah knew perfectly well that no meeting with the enemy could be productive because, so far as Nehemiah was concerned, his priority was non-negotiable. There are many such things we have to face, the truth of the inerrancy of Scripture, for instance, or any of the other great cardinal doctrines of the Christian faith. There is no point in even discussing them with the enemies of the gospel since we have no room for compromise on any of these things.

Now let us note The Parallel, for this whole story can be lifted from its Old Testament setting and put down in a New Testament one—similar but profoundly more significant. It is the same place we have in view, the city of Jerusalem, but a completely different period of time.

The scene is set on a skull-shaped hill not far from Jerusalem's wall, and the enemy is there in full force. Three crosses have been raised against the sky, and the anguish they represent can barely be imagined. On the center cross we see the Son of God. The mocking multitudes ignore the two thieves, for after all, they were just common criminals paying for their crimes. The malice of both the mob and the masters of Israel is directed toward the One who claimed to be the Son of God. The claim, they thought, was clearly incredible. But it made a good jest as well as a good test: "If thou be the Son of God," they said, "come down to us. Then we'll believe you." Nothing happened. No word passed His lips. Indeed, He had no need to speak. His answer had been on record for centuries. Nehemiah had spoken the words, and Jesus simply rested on them: "I am doing a great work," He might have said, "I cannot come down. Why should the work cease while I leave it and come down to you?"

And what a great work it was! He was securing eternal salvation for a countless multitude by bearing the sins of the world in His body on the tree. He was purchasing redemption for lost Adam's fallen race. He was working out a plan agreed upon by Father, Son and Holy Spirit before ever time began. Why, indeed, should the work cease while He came down from that cross to satisfy the idle curiosity of a disbelieving crowd? No! He stayed there, where He was, until the work was done. Then He spoke. "It is finished," He said. And so it was. We thank Him for it to this very day.

"BEHOLD, MY SORROW"

LAMENTATIONS 1:12

"Is it nothing to you, all ye that pass by? Behold and see if there be any sorrow like unto my sorrow, which is done unto me, wherewith the Lord hath afflicted me in the day of his fierce anger."

We think first of the Primary application of these words. They were spoken by Jeremiah, the weeping prophet of the Old Testament. All about him was a desolate, depopulated and devastated city. The Babylonians had torn it to pieces, destroyed its glorious temple, deported its people and defied its God. So much for all his preaching! He had been reviled and afflicted by his own people, and now he roamed the corpse-strewn ruins of Jerusalem abandoned to his grief. So great where his sorrows a special book of the Bible was set apart to record them, the book of Lamentations. Truly Jeremiah was a man of sorrows.

We think, next of the Peripheral application of these words. For there are others, whose stories are treasured up within the bounds of God's book, people who learned through sufferings.

There was <u>Joseph,</u> for instance. Doubtless, by the time of his mother's death, Joseph had learned to be afraid of his older brothers. They hated him and could not speak peaceably to him. It is doubtful, however, that, cautious as he had become, that he was prepared for their final, united onslaught on him. He never thought he would be flung into a pit, his princely mantle torn from his shoulders, his fate fiercely debated by his brothers and with murder in the scales, the prospect of being hauled from the pit and sold into slavery in a foreign land never occurred to him. And then, in that faraway land, to be falsely accused and flung into prison and left there to rot! Such were the sufferings of Joseph.

Then there was <u>Jonah</u>. True, he brought his suffering on himself; but it was none the less real and terrible for all that. We can scarcely imagine the horror of his situation, to be swallowed alive and lost in the vast interior of a whale. To be in the dark, awash with the debris of a great sea creature's meals. To be scorched by its gastric juices, to be overwhelmed by the heat and suffocated by the smell. No wonder he called it "the belly of hell." And the torment went on for three days and three nights. Certainly Jonah came very near to death. Such were the sufferings of Jonah.

And what about <u>Job</u>? Sorrow after sorrow surged in upon his soul. Wealth gone, health gone, family gone, friends gone—until he felt that God Himself had become his enemy. And all this for no apparent reason and, it seemed, with no foreseeable end. His friends hotly debated the cause of Job's suffering and concluded they could only be explained in terms of some horrendous secret sin in Job's life—a conclusion he vehemently denied. Nobody divined the true cause of Job's torment, or the triumphant conclusion that would he his. Such were the sufferings of Job.

Which brings us to the <u>Prophetic</u> application of these words: "Is it nothing to you, all ye that pass by? Behold and see if there be any sorrow like unto my sorrow which is done unto me, wherewith the Lord hath afflicted me in the day of His fierce anger?" For the sufferings of Jeremiah and the sufferings of Joseph and the sufferings of Jonah and the sufferings of Job all pale before the sufferings of JESUS. Like Jeremiah, He wept over Jerusalem, like Joseph, He came unto His own; and His own received Him not. Like Jonah, all God's waves and billows passed over Him; and He cried in utter desperation and desolation in total darkness. And, like Job, His sufferings were all undeserved. There was no sorrow like His.

Who can even begin to imagine the sufferings of Jesus when He, who knew no sin, was made sin for us. Only God can know the full measure of that. Well might we borrow the language of the old hymn:

"Oh, make me understand it,
Help me to take it in,
What it meant for Thee, the Holy One,
To take away my sin."

I FELL AT HIS FEET AS DEAD: THE UNKNOWABLE ONE
REVELATION 1:13-16

John had known Him, long years ago, before ever His name became a household word. He had often seen Him in His peasant homespun, seamless robe. He had seen Him at work in the carpenter's shop, every saw cut, joint and decoration a masterpiece. He had caught a glimpse of the glory that was His on the holy mount. But there had never been anything like this, the vision glorious on the Patmos Isle. He fell at His feet as dead. He tries to tell us what he saw, tries to translate into human speech the marvels and mysteries of heaven. The best he can do is to fall back on symbols. There were ten separate details that were impressed upon his soul.

First, he saw the Lord as The Unknowable One. So much about Him was concealed. "He was clothed," John says, "in a garment down to the foot."

John remembered the robe that Jesus wore the day that He was crucified. That robe had been flung over His shoulders and back, wet with His blood from the thongs of the scourge. The soldiers rolled their dice to see who would have it as his prize.

Our attention is drawn to the garment, the seamless robe Jesus wore when He was crucified. There were five articles of dress—the headpiece, the sandals, the outercovering and the girdle, and the seamless robe of more value than all the rest. There were four soldiers. Four soldiers were assigned to each cross. They had stood stolidly by as Christ was scourged.

47

They had laughed with derision as Christ was mocked, in an imitation robe and wearing a crown of thorns.

But now the horseplay was over. The mocking purple was snatched away and his own clothes tossed to Him. He put on the robe. Blood from the scourging stained it. Perhaps John could remember the first time Jesus put it on, a present from His mother, perhaps, or an aunt, or a friend. John would certainly remember this last time He put it on, over His tortured body, in Pilate's judgment hall.

Our attention is drawn to the gamblers. The four soldiers assigned to Christ's cross made short work of the shoes, the girdle, the head gear, and the outer covering. But what about the robe. It was too valuable to be torn in pieces and divided up. So they found their dice and gambled for it. So careless, so callous is this world towards the Son of God.

But then after all, there was the goal. For this very act of gambling was of God. It is the subject of prophesy (Ps. 22:18) and of history (Matt. 27:35). Doubtless the winning soldier cleansed the robe, and stuffed it in his bag. Then he marched off with it into oblivion. And it is a good thing he did, or an apostate church in a later age would have made a relic of it and put it in a shrine with legends of its imagined healing power to be venerated and worshipped and displaced God's Son.

Some 730 years before, Isaiah described another robe, one not worn, as yet, on earth. He tells us that, at His coming again, He will come striding up from Edom, His garment red with blood from treading out the vintage where the grapes of wrath were stored.

But John, it is, who sees beyond all this. He sees "this same Jesus." And the first of ten awesome sights is the sight of the Savior, once again arrayed in a robe. All he saw was His head, His hands, His feet. The robe concealed the rest. That all-concealing robe reminds us how little we know of Him.

What did He do between His birth and His baptism? We do not know. What did He do day by day, hour by hour, in the years of His ministry? We do not know. The Gospels themselves are mere fragments, hardly more than memos. John's, for instance, devotes half of its length to the events of one week. Only thirty-six miracles are recorded in the Gospels. He performed thousands.

The seamless robe He wore when here spoke symbolically of humanity. There is something very human about a man wearing a robe. The robe John saw concealed most of the all-mysterious person of the now ascended Son of the living God. There is so much more about Him yet to be revealed. The book of Revelation is "the Apocalypse," the "unveiling" of Jesus Christ. But, when we reach the end of it and John puts down his pen, we still feel that there remains very much more to be said. Our few short years of time enable us to merely touch the hem of that garment down to the foot. It will take us all eternity to know Him as we ought.

I FELL AT HIS FEET AS DEAD: THE UNEMOTIONAL ONE
REVELATION 1:13

John was down there in the dust of the marble quarry, flat on his face, as one already dead. He raised his eyes a little and saw the hem of a garment. He raised his head. All he could see was that robe. Almost all else was concealed. The One at whose feet he lay was THE UNKNOWABLE One. Very little could be seen of Him, still less could be really known.

As he gazed higher, he saw that this One was "girded across the breast with a golden girdle." He was THE UNEMOTIONAL One. The breast is the seat of the emotions, as the head is the seat of the intellect. The girdle symbolizes restraint. The girdle was worn in John's day to hold back a person's flowing robes, to restrain them lest they should get in the way. More, the girdle John saw was a golden girdle. Gold is a biblical symbol for God. In the tabernacle, for instance, the boards were made of acacia wood, the common, gnarled and twisted wood of the desert; but they were overlaid with gold. The wood spoke of the Lord's down-to-earth humanity; the gold spoke of His deity. The golden girdle John saw, wound around the heart of Jesus, draws our attention to the fact that His emotions are now not only restrained, they are Divinely restrained, held back by God.

It is not, of course, as though the Lord Jesus cannot feel. Of course, He can! He is our great High Priest, even at this moment, "touched with the feelings of our infirmities." More! He has been described as "a man of sorrows, acquainted with grief." He taught His disciples that they should rejoice with those who rejoice and weep with those who weep. Nobody knew this better than John. It is no accident that the first miracle of Christ's ministry, recorded in John's gospel, was performed at a wedding and the last one at a funeral—life's gladdest and life's saddest hours. Yes, indeed! The Lord Jesus is deeply moved in His heart by the terrible things sin has done in this world. Three times we read that He wept. He wept at the tomb of Lazarus, for an individual. He wept on the Mount of Olives, for a Christ-rejecting nation. He wept and wept in dark Gethsemane for all the sons of Adam's ruined race.

And there was joy, too, "joy unspeakable and full of glory." It was for the joy set before Him He endured the cross. He stood with the cheering section of glory to add His joyful welcome when Stephen, battered but triumphant, burst into glory.

But now all that kind of thing is put under Divine restraint. All emotion is held in check. He is about to begin His "strange work" and launch an offensive of judgment and wrath upon this world. No wonder all feelings are now firmly held back. Emotion must neither be allowed to feed His fury or to cause pity to mitigate His wrath. Let all men be advised the mercy seat has now become the judgment seat. The hour of His wrath has come. There are no scenes in the Bible more sobering or more solemn than this, or more terrible than those about to begin.

I FELL AT HIS FEET AS DEAD: THE INIMPEACHABLE ONE
REVELATION 1:14

John was still at His feet as one dead. Often, in past days, he had leaned on this One's breast. But not now. Not even the blinding vision on the Holy Mount, when Moses and Elijah appeared, and Jesus was transfigured, remotely resembled this. The One in whose dread presence he now lay prostrate on the ground was the unknowable One. He was the unemotional One, girt around the breast with a golden girdle. He ventures another look. His head and His hair, he sees, were white, like wool, like snow. He is also the UNIMPEACHABLE One, the Holy One, holy beyond all thought.

It was not thus that John remembered Him, with hair whither than the driven snow. Nor was it thus that the Shulamite described her beloved— her beloved who so majestically pictures our Beloved.

Solomon, we remember, had abducted the Shulamite and had sought to overwhelm her with his wealth and words. Unable to achieve his ends, he turned her over to the court women, hoping that these harem beauties might persuade her to yield her affections to him. No way! Her heart and her affections were already engaged to another, to her beloved shepherd. The exasperated court women burst out, "And what is thy beloved more than another beloved?" What does He have that Solomon, prince of this world, does not have? The Shulamite described Him: "My beloved is white and ruddy," she said. "He is the chiefest among ten thousand. His head is of the most fine gold, his locks are bushy and black as a raven." Thus she described her beloved—and our Beloved, as seen through Old Testament eyes.

What happened to turn those locks of His from the blackness of a raven's wing to the whiteness of the virgin snow?

In the IMAX version of Niagara Falls, we are shown the first person ever to go over the Falls in a barrel. It was a woman, and one of the few to survive. She took a small, black kitten with her in the barrel to be her companion on the nightmare ride. When they emerged, the kitten had turned white. It was the movie maker's way of reminding us that some horrific experience can turn black hair white.

"His locks," said the Shulamite, "are bushy and black as a raven." His head and His hair are white, like snow," says John. Something of a horrifying nature must have happened. And so it did—CALVARY.

That ordeal had ever been before Him, from before the foundation of the world. It assumed more concrete form when, as a boy of twelve, on the occasion of His first Passover in Jerusalem, He contemplated the death of the Lamb. It took a new nightmare turn in Gethsemane when, as the poet puts it:

> "Three times, alone in the garden
> He prayed, 'Not My will but Thine —'
> He shed no tears for His own griefs
> But wept drops of blood for mine."

And then it burst upon Him in all its horror at the place called Calvary when He who knew no sin was made sin for us and when He, the source of all life, tasted death for everyone.

Since then, His hair has been white. Whenever we look at Him, through all the endless ages yet to be, that snowy hair will remind us how greatly He must have loved us to suffer so.

I FELL AT HIS FEET AS DEAD: THE UNDECEIVABLE ONE

REVELATION 1:14

Perhaps it was His eyes which struck the prone apostle with the greatest terror "for," he said, "His eyes were like a flame of fire." He saw Him now as the UNDECEIVABLE One, able to penetrate through all subterfuge as white hot concentrated heat can slice through steel. Fire can consume suns and stars and mighty galaxies. Nothing can hide from fire. When He lived on earth, as John remembered Him, He wept with those that wept, His eyes were a fountain of tears. No more. They are now a flame of fire.

Charles Dickens tells us what happened to the violent robber, Bill Sikes, after he had murdered Nancy, the woman who loved him. "At length," he said, "the sun shed its light into the room where the murderer cowered still, afraid to take his eyes off the corpse." Once he threw a rug over it, but then he imagined those staring eyes moving toward him, so he tore the rug away. With the first light of day the criminal fled, but the eyes followed him. Indeed, it seemed to him that the corpse itself followed him, but especially "the eyes."

In the end they killed him. The murderer was cornered in the attic of a house with a howling mob outside and no place to go. Only one hope remained. He opened the window and crawled out on the roof. The crowd saw him and let out a roar. The criminal tied a rope around a chimney, made a loop in it and passed it over his head. He intended to place it under his arms and lower himself down to the river. But then he saw the eyes. With a yell of terror, he lost his balance. The rope around his neck ran swiftly through its coils, and he was jerked violently to his death. He swung lifeless between heaven and earth, killed by those wide-staring eyes.

But those were only the eyes of a murdered girl. Who can imagine the dread terror which will be inspired in all, at last, by the eyes of a murdered Christ but now resurrected? What about those eyes that are as a flame of fire, those eyes that see everything and miss nothing?

I remember the text that hung upon my boyhood, bedroom wall: "Thou God seest me," it said. The words were first spoken by poor, ill-treated, runaway Hagar when God came to her as once He had come to Abraham. It was a comforting thought to her, that God saw her. It was intended to be a comforting thought to me. But it had another and a different message—"Thou God seest me." It brought to memory my boyish sins, sins that God saw. It ceased to be a comforting text; it became a condemning text.

"Thou God seest me!" It will be the tormented cry of the lost, at the Great White Throne, as they realize they have no secrets and no hiding place. In vain do they call on the mountains and hills to fall on them and blot out the terror of those all-seeing eyes. And those eyes of His will follow them out into a lost eternity, haunting them forever and ever. But, as for us who have come to love the Lord, the words, "Thou God seest Me," are transformed by the chemistry of Calvary. They threaten us no more. They thrill us now. He sees!

I FELL AT HIS FEET AS DEAD:
THE UNDETERRABLE ONE
REVELATION 1:15

John looked away from those fiery eyes, and his gaze dropped to the Master's feet. "His feet," he says, "were like burnished brass when it had been made to glow in a furnace." Brass is a common symbol in scripture for judgment. Nothing can halt the march of those feet when once He rises up to judge the world. He is the UNDETERRABLE One. John saw those feet when they were nailed to a cross. He saw them in the upper room on the day Christ rose. He saw them step from the brow of Olivet into the sky. But we must pause and trace their ordained path.

Those feet broke through the silence of a past eternity and awoke the echoes of the everlasting hills. A thousand billion galaxies were but cobblestones beneath them, mere pebbles on His pathway across the vastness of the universe.

But listen now! Those feet step out of eternity into time. And lo! They have become baby feet. For the path He chose led through the confines of a virgin's womb to a human body just like ours. Baby feet they were, challenging a mother's busy fingers to knit little booties and things to keep them warm.

And now they have become the busy feet of a boy, running here and there, climbing trees, splashing in a water hole, walking back and forth to school, hopping along to the synagogue, and on into the carpenter's shop.

What blessed feet they were! They took Him through Samaria when anyone else would have gone miles out of their way, around and across Jordan in order not to go through Samaria. But He knew of a well there at Sychar and of a woman, shopworn and weary, a woman He wanted to meet and bless and transform. Then on to other people in other places—to Nicodemus in Jerusalem, to Jairus in Galilee, to Zacchaeus near Jericho. Those blessed feet of His were ever on the go until He had visited each corner of the Promised Land, taking Him by way of Calvary to the haunted halls of Hades, and then on back to earth, to heaven, and to home.

But hark! All is now changed. Those feet are now like burnished brass. Their tramp shakes the earth to its foundation, in ways the Psalms describe (Ps. 18, 29)

For down here on earth the tramp of other feet are heard. The teeming millions of the East break away from the Empire of the Beast. They mobilize men by the million and march them to Megiddo. The West is mobilized in response. The tramp of western armies is heard across many an ancient battlefield. They, too, are marching to Megiddo.

The issue in this "war to end all war" is simple enough. Who will rule the world—East or West? So the stage is set for conflict and carnage such as the world has never known in all its long and war-filled past.

But suddenly, above all the noise and din on earth, there comes a terrifying sound—marching feet on high, feet of burning brass, feet shod now to trample out the vintage of the earth. The heavens rend asunder with a roar. Satan's hosts on high are swept aside, of no account. The Lord is passing through the heavens on His way to earth. The hour of His wrath has come. God-hating men, Christ-rejecting men, gathered in the cockpit of the world, are face to face with doom. Those trampling feet make short work of the millions at Megiddo, and move on their relentless way to touch down on Olivet. It splits asunder with a roar. The Lord has come at last! None can bar His way. Heaven is His throne, earth His footstool—and every knee shall bow to own Him Lord.

The whole creation groans, anticipating the coming of its absent Lord, straining towards that day, looking forward to the day when He, at last, will tread the earth once more.

I FELL AT HIS FEET AS DEAD: THE UNANSWERABLE ONE
REVELATION 1:15

There John lay, still lying at those feet, as one dead. Only now sight gives way to sound. He hears a voice. Oh, how often he had heard that voice in those far-off Galilean days, the voice of Jesus, sometimes sweeter than the honeycomb, saying to the sinful woman, "Neither do I condemn thee, go and sin no more;" sometimes softer than the whisper of the wind in the willows, saying to the dying thief, "This day thou shalt be with Me in paradise;" and sometimes sterner than cold steel, saying to His disciples, "One of you is a devil." How John remembered that voice! Even His enemies felt its force. The Sermon on the Mount. The mystery parables. The discourse on the Mount of Olives. Truly, "never man spake like this Man!"

But now all is changed. "His voice," John says, "is as the voice of many waters." He is the UNANSWERABLE One. On the Canadian side of Niagara Falls the visitor can go down an elevator shaft to a long corridor which brings him to a platform underneath the Falls. Some fourteen million people a year come to see these awesome Falls. Every minute 34.5 million gallons of water go over the edge into the boiling cauldron below.

It is a place of roaring cataracts, swirling whirlpools, towering, rocky banks. And oh! How that sound of many waters drowns all other sounds. The Indians called it, "the place of thundering waters." Such is now the voice of Jesus preparing for judgment. There will be no discussion, no debate next time He speaks.

One of the mysteries of this present age is His silence. A silence absolute and prolonged—for nearly two thousand years. But it is not the silence of indifference. It is the silence of a great sabbatical rest. The Son of God has died at the hands of man. God might well have reacted in wrath, with a roar like thunder, with a shout, with the voice of the archangel and with the trump of doom. Instead, there was a silence, a silence which says that the way is open still for even the guiltiest to draw near and be forgiven.

Little do people realize what they are asking for when they challenge God to break that silence. He will break it one of these days and when He does it will mean the withdrawal of the amnesty, the end of the day of grace, the dawn of the day of wrath.

So John lay there, as that dread voice, like the thundering waters of Niagara, drowned out all other sound. The voice of the returning Christ will silence all words of ours, and will make even the thoughts of the mind to be confused. It will be the prelude to wrath. The silence will have been broken at long last and woe betide the world! Every mouth will be stopped. The whole world, guilty before God, will be judged. With fury unimagined, the apocalypse will come. Then, when even all that noise is stilled, lost men will find themselves standing exposed, ashamed and silenced, as the words of accusation and doom thunder and roar in their ears. John could find no other words to describe what will happen when God speaks again—"His voice is as the voice of many waters," he says. And leaves it at that.

I FELL AT HIS FEET AS DEAD: THE UNPARALLELED ONE

REVELATION 1:16

Still on his face, John ventured a further look at the awesome One who stood beside him. "And in His right hand He held seven stars," John said. He was the UNPARALLELED One, the One who rules the stars. Who but God alone could do such a thing? Take our own sun, for instance, it is a moderate star, numbered neither among the stellar giants or the stellar dwarfs. It weights 2.2 billion, billion, billion tons. It contains 99.86% of all the substance in our solar system. From birth to death, solar scientists affirm, the sun has a lifespan of about ten billion years. One second of the sun's energy is equal to thirteen million times the annual mean electricity consumption of the United States. John saw the Lord holding seven such stars in His right hand. That, of course, amounts to nothing to One who includes omnipotence among His attributes. Let us beware of a concept of our Lord which is too small.

It is evident, of course, whatever lessons we can draw from such a view of the might and magnificence of our Lord, that the Holy Spirit does not intend us to take this literally. It is clearly symbolic. Indeed, we are not left to speculate about this because the Spirit Himself interprets the symbolism. The lampstands which John saw represented seven churches, churches which existed in John's day, churches he knew well and which he had often visited in days gone by. The stars symbolized the angels of those churches.

There are various ranks and responsibilities among the angels. Satan's fallen angels include principalities and powers, the rulers of this world's darkness and wicked spirits in high places. God's angels include thrones and dominions, high dignitaries of heaven. There are countless legions of messenger angels, such as Gabriel, martial angels, led by Michael, and ministering angels, who attend to the needs of God's people in enemy territory on earth.

Children have their guardian angels who report all child abuse directly to God. Christians have their angels—both Peter and Paul saw theirs. Christ had His ministering angels—we see, for instance, them caring for

Him at the close of His temptation in the wilderness, and after His agony in Gethsemane. Now we learn that <u>churches</u> have their guardian angels. (There is a passing confirmation of this in 1 Corinthians 11, where Paul tells ministering women to cover their heads "because of the angels."

Each of the seven churches of Asia had its angel. Each one reported directly to Christ, the Head of the Church. He controls their activities and holds them in His right hand, the hand of power. Churches need the help of these angels for ours is a spiritual warfare. Our ministering angels draw the line beyond which Satan and his evil spirits cannot go. Herod, for instance, was smitten when he went too far. We should be thankful for these powerful allies in our continuing battle against the forces of sin.

I Fell At His Feet As Dead: The Unconquerable One
Revelation 1:16

Still in his prone position, John ventured to lift his eyes higher. "Out of His mouth," he said, came a sharp, two-edged sword." He was the UNCONQUERABLE One.

The sword is first seen, of all places, in connection with the garden of Eden. The fall had taken place, and the world had suddenly become a wild and wicked place. The sentence of death has been pronounced upon Adam and his posterity, though there would be a stay of execution for some for many years. Thorns and thistles were already staking their claim to the earth, and the lion's roar and the wolf's snarl were suddenly full of menace.

The guilty pair, banished from Eden, thought nostalgically of their former safe, Edenic home. Perhaps they could go back and (sudden, sinful thought) perhaps they could gain access to the tree of life and circumvent the sentence of death. There, ahead of them, was the garden gate. They made their way towards it. Then they saw one of the cherubim, an angelic being, with a drawn sword in his hand, barring their way. Distant death suddenly became threatened, present death. God was not going to allow them to eat of the tree of life, for then they would have lived forever in their sins, deathless as the angels and sinful as the hosts of hell. They turned away, haunted by the memory of that flaming sword.

The next time we see the sword, it is through the eyes of a young prophet, one of the last of the Old Testament prophets, Zechariah by name. "Awake O sword against my shepherd," he said, "smite the shepherd and the sheep shall be scattered. . ." Centuries later his words were fulfilled. At Calvary the sword of the living God awakened, and its blade burned and blazed in the hand of God. It was plunged into the heart of Jesus. The downward thrust of that terrible, swift sword was not arrested. It was driven deep into the Savior's soul. When it was withdrawn, the blood of Jesus, gushing forward, became a crimson tide, a fountain for uncleanness opened up for all.

But we are not yet done with that sword. John on Patmos, prostrate on the ground, saw it coming out of the mouth of the Son of God. The language, of course, is symbolic. Paul says that "the sword of the Spirit" is "the Word of God." God is now about to wreak vengeance on this world and on the wicked race which murdered His Son.

The scene changes. We are at Megiddo. The armies of the world, East and West, face each other, armed with weapons of mass destruction. With a roar, the heavens split wide, and the Son of God appears. That symbolic sword comes out of His mouth; He speaks. One word from Him, and all is over! He speaks, and down they go! That sharp, two-edged sword has done its work. Now there will be peace upon this planet for a thousand years. The sword can rest at last.

I FELL AT HIS FEET AS DEAD: THE UNAPPROACHABLE ONE
REVELATION 1:16

John raised <u>his</u> head one more time, this time to glance at the face of Jesus. He turned away blinded, dazzled. "His face," he said, "was like the sun shining in its strength"—the UNAPPROACHABLE One.

John well remembered the face of Jesus, the Jesus he had known, probably since boyhood days, the Jesus whose disciple he had become. In those days, He had been the most approachable of men. Little children sensed it and climbed up on His knee. Anyone could come. Aristocratic Nicodemus could come, the woman at the well could come. Simon the leper could come. Poor, blind Bartimeus could come. Rich man, poor man, beggar man and thief, all could come. And His beaming face made them welcome and put them all at ease.

But that was then. And this was now. John was looking at "this same Jesus" whom he and the others had seen ascend bodily into heaven. But, oh! how different! Now He was as unapproachable as the sun. We cannot even look directly into the face of the sun, shining in its strength. We certainly cannot approach it. John, who had been the closest disciple, the dearest friend of this One whose face now resembled the sun, was at His feet as dead.

Think for a moment of the sun, shining in its strength. It has a diameter of 864,000 miles. The core of the sun is subject to inconceivable pressure—a million, million pounds per square inch. The only thing which keeps the sun's core from collapsing and solidifying is its energy—energy almost beyond belief, energy sufficient to raise the internal temperature to 25 million degrees Fahrenheit by nuclear fusion, similar to that which takes place when a hydrogen bomb is exploded. The energy resulting from this process eventually reaches the surface of the sun. It then radiates into space. The sun, we are told, shines with a constant power of 380 million billion billion watts. Sunlight travels at the speed of light and takes eight minutes to travel from the sun to earth. Solar flares, brilliant flashes of light in the solar atmosphere, sometimes produce energies equal to a billion hydrogen bombs. Such is the sun.

One glimpse of the face of Jesus, and all John could think of was the sun. Such will the face of Jesus be towards His foes, when He comes again. Men will scream in terror at the sight. And well they might.

But for us, it will be a smiling face, aglow with all the light of heaven, with radiant love for His own.

I FELL AT HIS FEET AS DEAD: THE UNCHANGEABLE ONE

REVELATION 1:17

Thus John saw Him as he lay face down in the dust, overwhelmed at the heavenly vision. He was terrified. And no wonder. Let us put it all together. The One in whose dread presence He was, filled him with fear.

1. He was the UNKNOWABLE One, "clothed with a garment down to the foot."

2. He was the UNEMOTIONAL One, "girded across the breast with a golden girdle."

3. He was the UNIMPEACHABLE One, "His head and His hairs were white like wool, like snow."

4. He was the UNDECEIVABLE One, "His eyes were like a flame of fire."

5. He was the UNDETERRABLE One, "His feet were like burnished brass when it has been made to glow in a furnace."

6. He was the UNANSWERABLE One, "His voice is as the voice of many waters."

7. He was the UNPARALLELED One, "In His right hand He held seven stars."

8. He was the UNCONQUERABLE One, "And out of His mouth came a sharp, two-edged sword."

9. He was the UNAPPROACHABLE One, "And His face was like the sun, shining in its strength."

But there was one thing more.

10. He was the UNCHANGEABLE One, for "He laid His right hand upon me, saying unto me, Fear not: I am the first and the last: I am

He that liveth and was dead; and behold I am alive forevermore . . . and have the keys of hell and of death."

It was "this same Jesus" after all! The terrifying appearance is for His foes, not His friends. That gentle touch, that gracious voice! It was the same. There was nothing to fear—not even death itself, for He now holds the keys of death and hell. Paul calls death the last enemy. Spurgeon says, "If death is the last enemy, then leave him till last." Jesus says, "Leave him to Me!"

John never feared again. See him there in glory, midst scenes of grandeur. All about him are the crowned royalties of heaven. There he is, one lone man. Tears! Yes! Sorrow that not one man is fit to govern the globe? Yes! Fear? Oh no!

Now he sees the four horsemen of the Apocalypse ride forth. Stars fall from the sky, earthquakes rock the globe, the mighty men of earth shake in their shoes. Not John! His Friend, Jesus holds all the keys.

The seven trumpets blare, and now the devil rules the earth. An angel calls down woes upon the world, and John stands amidst it all unafraid.

A mighty angel holds a little book. John is told to go and take it. "Give it to me," he says to this mighty, majestic lord of another world. And, at once, the book is surrendered into John's outstretched hand. Bitterness? Yes! Nausea? Yes! Fear? No. What is there to fear? He has been told: "Fear not." He needs to be told it only once. The most horrendous, end-time judgments leave him unmoved. He is immortal till his work is done. And so are we. "Fear not," Jesus says, "I have the keys."

LO I COME
HEBREWS 10:7-9

"Lo I come (in the volume of the book it is written of me) to do Thy will, O God." This is Christmas as seen from the standpoint of eternity. The context shows that, from the beginning, two things would be needed to rescue fallen man—a book and a body. Both are mentioned here.

First, the BOOK. It took some four thousand years to write that Book. It involved people drawn from various walks of life. It is a book of <u>startling prophecies</u>, many of them focused on the two comings of Christ. It is a book of <u>symbolic pictures</u>, pictures we call "types," coded prophecies of things to come. Take one, for example—the slaying of the Passover Lamb.

The lamb had to be taken on the tenth day of the first month of the Jewish year. The Lord arrived in Jerusalem on that very day—the tenth day if Nisan. The lamb had to be tethered on the day it was bought. On that day the Sanhedrin bought Jesus from Judas for thirty pieces of silver. The Lord stayed close to Jerusalem from then on, under the eyes of Judas. Each night He went out to nearby Bethany, each day He came back to Jerusalem. That was the length of His tether. Like the Old Testament paschal lamb, He was kept under constant observation.

The Passover was killed on the fourteenth day of the first month—the very day of the crucifixion—"the preparation of the Passover," the day was called. The lamb was killed "between the two evenings" (Ex. 12:6). Josephus identifies this as being from the sixth hour to the ninth hour—that was when the Jews killed their lamb. And that was when they killed Him, the true paschal Lamb. So, to the year, to the month, to the day, to the hour, God's Lamb was slain—such is the accuracy of the Book.

Which brings us to THE BODY. "Sacrifice and offering Thou wouldest not, but a body hast Thou prepared for me." These are the very words Jesus spoke as recorded by the Spirit of God. The body was necessary so that God the Son could become the Son of man. It was necessary, too, so that He could be offered as a sacrifice, once and for all.

It was "prepared," the Holy Spirit says. The Greek word is <u>katartizo</u>. It means "to mend." It is used of James and John mending their nets. The human body, damaged by the fall, subject to disease, deformity and death, was "mended" for Jesus. His was a perfect body, one completely undamaged by sin. It was free from congenital weakness and from latent weakness. He was free from sin, free from sickness, free from accidents, free from all bodily harm—"a Lamb without blemish and without spot".

It was the Holy Spirit who went to work in the womb of the woman, to create that body. He guided the creation of the six trillion cells which made up that holy body. When, finally, it was finished, Jesus was born and the angels came down in droves to gaze upon the marvel of it all.

Jesus lived in that body, on this planet in space, for thirty-three and a half years. Then He gave that body to be broken. We see that body bowed to the earth and shaken with sobs in Gethsemane. We see it bruised and buffeted at Gabbatha and scourged to the bone in Pilate's hall. We see it crowned with thorns, smitten and spat upon. We see it, arms outstretched to save, spiked to a cross at Golgotha. Finally we see it in its grave. It was sealed and secured. It slept in total incorruption. And, on the third day, it burst forth from the tomb. Now it is enthroned on high.

So a Book has been written. A body has been risen. And now we have a Savior which is Christ the Lord! THAT is Christmas from heaven's point of view. Blessed be God our God.

"AND THE WORD WAS MADE FLESH"
JOHN 1:14

"And the Word was made flesh and dwelt among us, and we beheld His glory, the glory as of the only begotten of the Father, full of grace and truth."

At once our attention is drawn to His GODHEAD. And also to the mystery of His person. "God is a spirit," Jesus told the woman at the well. As the second Person of the Godhead, so was He; but He was also "made flesh." That is to say, He assumed humanity and inhabited a body of flesh and blood. Paul expresses the awesomeness of that. He says: "In Him dwelt all the fullness of the Godhead, bodily."

"In the beginning," John explains, "was the Word." That does not refer to a start but a state. We go back to the beginning of things, and He was there.

"And the Word was God," John continues. He was "with God," a separate person within the Godhead. The reference is to His essential deity. The verb "was" is not in the past tense but in the imperfect tense.

"The same was in the beginning with God," John adds, taking us back before the creation. "All things were made by Him," he declares, naming Him as the Creator of the entire universe.

And, finally, we come to this: "The Word was made flesh." God became Man. There now lives a Man who is God. Paul says: "Being in the form of God He thought it not robbery to be equal with God." However, "He took upon Him the form of a servant." He was, "made in the likeness of men." And He was, "found in fashion as a man." (Phil. 2:6-8) There are enough mysteries there to occupy us for all eternity.

John now turns to the Lord's GRACE. He came and dwelt among us. The word he used means that "He pitched His tent," among us, literally, He tabernacled among us—the very word takes us back a millennium and a half to the days of Moses. For God told Moses He had decided to come down to earth and live with His people. What grace! He came from the mansions of glory, from a rainbow-circled throne. Countless angels in robes of light hung upon His words and rushed to do His will. Yet down to earth He came to "tabernacle" with men, to dwell in a tent in the midst of His pilgrim people, all the way from Sinai to the Promised Land. Isn't that just like Him?

Finally, we catch a glimpse of HIS GLORY. There was nothing beautiful about the outside covering of the Old Testament tabernacle, but inside it was all gleaming gold, brilliant color and costly fabric—all ablaze with the light of another world.

Similarly, the glory of the Lord Jesus was a hidden glory. His majestic glory, the glory He had with His Father before the world began, was rarely seen. He had emptied Himself of that. John caught just a glimpse of it on the Transfiguration Mount (Matt. 17:1-2). His moral glory was evident to all who had eyes to see. John saw it and describes it as "the glory as of the only begotten of the Father, full of grace and truth." Grace is the overflow of God's love. Truth is the substance of God's Law. Both were in perfect balance in Christ. For those who had eyes to see, and ears to hear, that glory was their foretaste of heaven. Such is our Lord and our God.

LIGHT IS COME INTO THE WORLD
JOHN 3:19

"This is the condemnation," says John, "that light is come into the world, and men loved darkness rather than light because their deeds were evil"

(John 3:19). This verse lives on the same street in scripture as its famous neighbor, John 3:16, and only three verses down. It is a great text in its own right, despite the fact that we tend to overlook it. It takes us to the cradle, to the cross and to the courtroom.

First, the CRADLE: "Light is come into the world." That is John's description of the birth of Christ. Light! Light was the first thing God called into existence when He created the world. Everything about light is mysterious. It can pass unsullied through a dirty windowpane. Its speed is always constant, some 186,000 miles per second—regardless as to whether or not two sources of light are traveling towards each other or away from each other. It is the great invariable in a world of constant motion, shifting patterns, endless change.

Jesus, "the light of the world," is always the same. He is, "the same, yesterday, today, and forever." When on earth He treated all men with the same, unwavering honesty, love, holiness and courtesy. He loved the elder brother just as much as He loved the runaway prodigal. He loved that scheming scoundrel Caiaphas just as much as He loved the attentive Nicodemus.

At Bethlehem God wrapped up deity in humanity. He appeared as a little Babe, dressed in swaddling clothes, lying in a manger! Or, to follow John's approach, at Bethlehem God lit a little candle and light came into the world. Satan thought it would be a good thing to extinguish that light before it flooded all the world. He made sure he had his man in place, a monster by the name of Herod. But Herod's murderers arrived too late. The light had been removed to Egypt. Now that light is everywhere. It shows us where we are and what we are, how lost we are and how dark a place this world is.

Next comes the CROSS: "Men loved darkness rather than light because their deeds were evil." The Lord's goodness exposed their badness. His honesty exposed their hypocrisy. His holiness exposed their wickedness. The authority of His teaching exposed the emptiness of theirs. Their answer was—get rid of Him. "This is your hour, and the power of darkness," He told them. They lied about Him, hired false witnesses against Him and crucified Him.

But, even on the cross, He demonstrated who He really was and who in fact, was in control. He put out the sun and total darkness reigned for three long hours. Then, as a parting gift, just before He died, He turned the light back on again. Then He died, and the true Light went out, not for a brief three hours, but for three whole days. Then, back He came! The darkness could not conquer the light after all.

Which brings us to the COURTROOM. Now He sits upon His Father's throne in heaven, in a light beyond the brightness of the noonday sun. One day the Christ-rejecting millions will be summoned to stand in the full blaze of that light, to be exposed, and then to be expelled to the blackness of darkness forever.

One last thought. We can shut the daylight out, but we cannot shut it in. Those who have come to the light and embraced the light will <u>shine</u>. They will "walk in the light as He is in the light," and they will find that "the path of the just is as a shining light that shineth more and more unto the perfect day." For just as the lost go out into the dark when death comes.

THE NAME OF MYSTERY
REVELATION 19:11-12

Heaven above rings with the shouts of "Hallelujah!" The sound awakes the echoes of the everlasting hills. Johns says that "much people in heaven" peal out those anthems of praise.

Much people in heaven! "Are there few that be saved?" the disciples once asked. It was a good question. The Lord said: Strait is the gate and narrow is the way that leadeth unto life, and few there be that find it." The kingdom parables (Matt.13) show similar seeming failure. Great deceptions hinder, if not halt, the onward march of God's activities on earth. But, when all God's purposes are done, He will be seen to "have the preeminence in <u>all</u> things." That surely includes numerical preeminence, too.

Perhaps the difference between "the few" referred to in one place and "the much people" referred to in another has to be found elsewhere in the onward march of His goodness and His grace, than in His purposes with the Church. For instance millions upon millions of people will be saved during the Tribulation age (Rev. 7). They will not be in the Church, though they will be in the Kingdom. And they will be in heaven. And so will all the little children of earth who were victims of infant mortality and never grew to reach the age of accountability surely, "of such is the kingdom of heaven."

The hallelujahs here, however, are heaven's spontaneous response to the sudden and total fall of Babylon and to the marriage supper of the Lamb. For that, too, is now ushered into history. Suddenly, without warning, heaven opens. The warring world looks up to see an invasion taking place from outer space. It is Jesus coming again!

The Holy Spirit now pauses to describe the awesome splendor of the returning Christ and draws our attention particularly, to the Names of Jesus. Every knee in the universe is soon to bow before the name of Jesus. But, for now, we are invited to consider some of his other names.

First, there is THE NAME OF MYSTERY. He has "a name written which no man knew but He Himself." From time to time in Scripture, during the onward march of things, God has broken into history to reveal Himself by many and varied names. But here is a name the purpose of which is not to reveal but conceal. This name suggests those deep and hidden depths in the nature, person and personality of Christ known to Him and His Father alone. One supreme mystery about the person of Christ is the fact that in Him dwells all the fullness of the Godhead bodily. "The heaven of heavens cannot contain Thee," Solomon said, "still less this temple I have built." Even less, we might think, the body of a babe. But, even as He was lying there, cradled in a woman's arms, He was upholding all things by the Word of His power. Countless galaxies roared and thundered overhead. It is He who guides them on their vast journeys. It is He who stokes the fierce fires which drive them at astounding speeds on orbits too great for us to grasp.

Think of the mystery of it! Deity is clothed in humanity; a Babe, lying in a Bethlehem barn, in infant attire, is the Ancient of days, arrayed in garments of light.

There He sits at His mother's knee, learning His alphabet, He who is the Alpha and the Omega, the very alphabet itself.

There He sits by a wayside well. Tired and thirsty He asks a woman for a drink—the One who engineered Niagara, and who pours its waters from lake to lake amid the awesome splendor of the falls.

We see Him accept the tribute of a small lad's lunch, He who, had He willed, could have turned stones to bread as simply as He once turned water into wine.

He was truly man, in every sense of the word; and He was truly God, over all, blessed forevermore. Never did He demonstrate His humanity at the expense of His deity. Never did He demonstrate His deity at the expense of His humanity. He always behaved as One who was both God and Man.

Think of the mystery of it! And remember He has a name to explain it all. That name written no less. It is a name held high, on a head now crowned with many crowns. But is "a name written that no man knew but He Himself."

THE NAME OF MINISTRY
REVELATION 19:13

"His Name is called the Word of God," the Holy Spirit adds. That brings us back to more familiar ground for "the Word of God" is John's favorite Name for Christ. It is THE NAME OF MINISTRY. It is the Name that mobilizes all that God is to take care of all that we are. The Word! When God wants to accomplish anything, He only has to speak. He speaks, and it is done.

When God decided to act in creation, He did so through His Word. The factual record of what happened is preserved for us by the Holy Spirit in Genesis 1. Ten times we read: "And God said." Here are God's first set of ten commandments, none of which have ever been broken. They stand in contrast with His second set of ten commandments (Ex. 20), none of which have ever been kept, in spirit and in truth—except by the incarnate Word Himself.

That Word was the active force in creation. "Light be!" He said. And light was. One word from Him, and an ocean seated itself in the sky, ascending and held there by the laws of evaporation, descending back down by the laws of precipitation. One word from Him, and life in myriad forms sprang into being and invaded every nook and cranny of the globe. What men call "nature" is merely His handmaid. Behind all of nature is the Word, and "the Word" is just another name for Jesus.

When God decided to act in revelation, He did so through His Word. He spoke! He wrote things down! Men and women, from all walks of life, became His instruments. Truth was revealed to them; and, inspired of God, they wrote and what they said was inerrant, the word of God.

When God decided to act in <u>redemption</u>, He did so through His word. The inspired word did well enough for several thousand years. It told us that a Redeemer was coming, One who could be "near of kin unto us" (Ruth 2:20). Now He has come. John describes him as "the Word made flesh." As we clothe our secret thoughts in words, and thus make them known, so the Word of God clothed in flesh to make plain to us what God is like. The Son of God became the son of man. He became the <u>incarnate</u> Word, our near Kinsman, related to us, by a common humanity so that He could redeem us as Boaz redeemed Ruth.

When the tabernacle furniture was made, special significance was attached to the ark of the covenant. It was a chest made of acacia wood (incorruptible wood designed by God to survive the hostile environment of the wilderness), and was overlaid with gold. The wood symbolized His sinless humanity, the gold symbolized His deity. Inside the ark was a pot of manna from the days of the wilderness years (to remind us how God meets our <u>material</u> needs), Aaron's rod that budded, a dead stick endued with life anew, bestowed by God (to remind us how God meets all our <u>spiritual</u> needs) and an unbroken copy of the law (to remind us how God meets all our <u>moral</u> needs). As that unbroken copy of the law reposed in the sacred ark, even so God's word, unbroken in thought, word or deed, rested in the heart of God's Son. It was what moved and motivated Him to magnify His Father and to minister to us.

When God finally acts in <u>retribution</u> it will be the same, He will act through His word. The Holy Spirit tells us of "the sword" that comes out of the mouth of the returning Christ (Rev. 19:15). A sword is used symbolically in scripture of God's word which is living and powerful and sharper than any two-edged sword (Eph. 6:17; Heb. 4:12). Thus He will deal with His foes. One word from Him and to a lost eternity they go, in a moment, in the twinkling of an eye, swifter than the lightning, surer than the dawn.

"His name is called the Word of God." It is the name that gets things done, a name that ministers to the glory of God and to the needs of men. That name is written on His blood-drenched robe. One day that Word will be the minister of His wrath. But for now the Word of God, incarnate in Christ, wears a shining face. It bids us know Him, whom to know is life eternal.

THE NAME OF MAJESTY
REVELATION 19:14-16

The Holy Spirit has another name to reveal. But first He paints a picture of the Lord. He is treading out the vintage where the grapes of wrath are stored. He has a sharp sword and a rod of iron! The sword tells us how He intends to <u>retake</u> the kingdom, the rod of iron how He intends to <u>rule</u> the kingdom. Already great Babylon has fallen (Rev. 18). Already earth's armies, East and West, are gathered at Megiddo (Rev. 16:13-16; 19:17-19). Already the birds of prey have been summoned to bury the multiplied millions of those soon to be dead. And now, descending the sky, comes the Invader from outer space and beyond. He is riding a great white horse (Rev.19:11). The King of Glory comes!

His vesture catches every eye. Blood red it is, and the battle not yet begun. And there, on that vesture a name is written: "King of Kings and Lord of Lords." Centuries ago Pilate, in bitter irony, wanting to irritate the Jews, wrote a mocking title and hung it over the head of the crucified Christ: "This is Jesus of Nazareth, the King of the Jews" it declared (Jn.19:19). It drew attention to the <u>Person</u> they despised—Jesus; and to the <u>Place</u> they despised—Nazareth; and to the <u>Prince</u> they despised. "King" indeed! They would rather have Caesar as king than Him, this meek Messiah, this weak Messiah, dying the death of a slave. They would rather have Barabbas for at least he had led an insurrection against Rome.

But the title was true just the same. He <u>was</u> the King of the Jews. An hour or two in the temple archives would have established that beyond all doubt. The record was available to all. His claim to the throne ran through the line of Joseph (who adopted Him) and through the line of Mary (who bore Him). It ran through David, Bathsheba and Solomon (Matt.1:6-16) and through David, Bathsheba and Nathan (Lk.3:23-31). His claim to the throne was crystal clear. The regal line through Joseph and the natural line through Mary climaxed and culminated in Him. The Lord, raised from the dead, is now the only possible heir to the throne of David. When the expected Jewish delegation arrived, demanding a change in the title now heralding the death of their King on a tree, Pilate sardonically declared:

"What I have written I have written." Thank you, Pilate, for the undeniable fact you proclaimed in that title, and thank you for the unexpected firmness you displayed. Well done! May it be to your credit in the day when the books are opened, and the dead judged according to their works, that at least, in this, you stood firm for the truth.

But here in Revelation 19 it is not the cross that is in view, but the <u>crown</u>. So, in defiance of all the powers of hell and all the massed millions of earth, one and all drawn to Megiddo for their doom, the full title is displayed: KING OF KINGS AND LORD OF LORDS. The hymn write well says:

> "Sinners in derision crowned Him
> Mocking thus the Savior's claim,
> Saints and angels crowd around Him
> Own His title, praise His Name."

The armies of the earth, led by their gods and their kings, energized by Satan and his demon hosts, redirect their weapons of mass destruction, aimed at each other, and point them at Him. They think, in their abysmal folly, that they can oppose Him. The second Psalm tells them otherwise. It tells of the terrible laughter of God, as He foresees and foretells this very event: "He that sitteth in the heavens shall laugh, the Lord shall have them in derision," the Holy Spirit says. That terrible laughter is the last thing they will hear on earth. It will awaken the echoes of the caverns of the damned. And now they know the truth—Jesus of Nazareth, the King of the Jews, is KING OF KINGS AND LORD OF LORDS.

INTO THE HOLIEST
HEBREWS 10:19-20

The veil of the Temple was a gorgeous curtain woven of the finest linen, dyed scarlet, blue and purple, as thick as a man's hand and embroidered with the forbidding figures of the cherubim. Its sole purpose was to provide a barrier between God and man. We notice four things brought to our attention in our text. We note What! Where! Why! and Who! "Boldness to enter,"—

that's <u>what</u>. "Into the Holiest," that <u>where</u>. "By the blood of Jesus,"—that's <u>why</u>. "Through the veil, that is to say, His flesh,"—that's <u>who</u>.

WHAT: We have "boldness to enter." And what boldness! No Jew would think of entering there. King Uzziah became a leper for trying to enter there. Boldness, yes! Presumption, no! But for us, in this age, to have boldness to enter where prophets, priests and kings all feared to tread, the entire protocol of the Old Testament had to be changed. Now we are invited in where, for Israel, the veil barred the way.

The story is told of a small boy who stood at the gate of Buckingham Palace, hoping to catch a glimpse of the king. A well-dressed man drove up and got out of his car. He glanced at the eager face of the boy. "Come with me," he said, extending his hand. The policeman stood aside, the gate was opened wide and a soldier presented arms. Up flights of stairs they went, through sumptuous apartments, on to a private suite, in the north wing, half a mile away from the kitchens. "This is my friend, Willy," said the man when, at last, they arrived in the presence of the King. "He wanted to see you. He took my hand so I brought him on in. Sonny, this is the king. He's my father. I'm Edward, Prince of Wales."

That is what! We have taken hold of a hand, the nail-scarred hand, of the King's own Son. So we have boldness to enter. He smoothes the way.

WHERE: "Into the Holiest!" It was the innermost shrine of the Temple where a thrice-holy God sat enthroned and where holiness shone in the blinding light of the Shekina. It was a holiness that could blaze out in judgment at any moment, as it did with Aaron's careless sons, Nadab and Abihu. These foolish men tried to approach God with their counterfeit fire. But Calvary has changed all that! We are now invited in, invited, even, to sit where the angel Gabriel dared only stand.

WHY:—The reason is simple. The blood of Jesus invites us in. The High Priest of old could enter inside the veil once a year, for a few fleeting moments, protected by the blood of a goat. We can come into the real holy of holies in heaven itself, protected by the blood of Jesus. That blood, shed at Calvary is now present on the mercy seat in the holy of holies in heaven.

WHO: "By a new and living way, through the veil, that is to say, His flesh . . ." That brings us back to Christ. "The Word was made flesh," John says, describing the incarnation of the Son of God. The flesh refers to His body which houses both His sinless humanity and His awesome deity. As the veil was first hung and then rent, so was the body of Jesus. It was hung on the cross and rent with a spear. At the same time, His body was rent on the <u>tree</u>, the veil was rent in the <u>temple</u>. A new and living way has been opened up for us into the immediate presence of a thrice-holy God! So let us boldly enter in.

WE SHALL BE LIKE HIM

I JOHN 3:1-2

"We shall be like Him!" John says, "for we shall see Him as he is." That points to LOVE beyond all human <u>comprehension</u> and to LIFE beyond all human <u>comparison</u>. John draws our attention to four features of that wondrous life.

There is, first, AN INDISPUTABLE FACT. "Beloved now are we the sons of God." There can be no room for uncertainty about that. God has said so, and God cannot lie. Now, right now, we <u>are</u> the sons of God. "Forever O Lord Thy Word is settled in heaven."

There is an old story about the lady who accepted Christ through reading John 3:16. The counsellor showed her where the verse was in her Bible and marked it for her. Later on that night, she had doubts. She felt the devil was attacking her newfound faith. She was a simple soul, but wise. She decided that the darkest place in the room was under the bed, so that was where the devil must be. She found John 3:16 in her Bible. She put her finger on the verse. She thrust the Bible under the bed. "Here," she said, "read it for yourself!" Now <u>ARE</u> WE (right <u>now</u>) "the sons of God." We can read it for ourselves. There can be no doubt.

There is, however, AN INFLUENCING RESTRICTION because there is something which is "not yet." John says: "It doth not yet appear what we shall be." Our thoughts are too dull, our minds too slow, our imaginations too poor, our experience too small and we have too little to go on for us to be able to grasp the wonders of the world to come. When Paul tried to describe what he had experienced when caught up to the third heaven, all he could say, when he came back down to earth, was "It is untranslatable!" (2 Cor. 12:4). When John tried to describe the wonders of the world to come, he resorted at once to symbolic language (Rev. 4,5). The Bible contains a strange mixture of things vividly real and hard as concrete, and things mystical, ethereal and beyond our grasp. God says, "Not yet!" when we try to probe too far.

There is also AN INDESCRIBABLE RESULT. "We shall be like Him," John says. Imagine! Like <u>Him</u>! For all the endless ages of eternity! Like Him in thought and word and deed, in body, soul and spirit! Like Him in character, conduct and conversation. We sing of our present earthly experience, of our longing to be like Him —

> *"Be like Jesus, this my song*
> *In the home and in the throng,*
> *Be like Jesus all day long,*
> *I would be like Jesus."*

At best we achieve only a vague resemblance to Him down here: but we <u>know</u> that when He shall appear, we shall be like Him.

Finally, there is AN INFALLIBLE REASON: "We shall be like Him for we shall see Him as He is!" John had once experienced the soul-thrilling rapture of such a vision. It was on the Mount of Transfiguration (Matt. 17:1-8) though he does not speak of it in his gospel. The synoptic writers had already told that story, the story of a vision of glory of the visitors from another world, and of a voice from heaven. John had been there along with Peter and James. He had seen the Lord's clothes ablaze with light, His face beaming like the sun. One day we are going to see Him just like that. We shall see Him as He is, in all the splendor of His humanity and in all the effulgence of His deity. Instantly, eternally, gloriously we shall be like Him. Well might John Nelson Darby write.[1]

> *"And is it so, I shall be Like Thy Son?*
> *Is this the grace that He for me has won?*
> *Wonder of wonders; thought beyond all thought*
> *In glory to His own blest likeness wrought*

Yes, it must be: Thy love had not its rest
Were Thy redeemed not with Thee fully blessed,
That loves not as the world but shares
All it possesses with its loved co-heirs."

---

¹Hymns of Worship (Truth and Praise, Inc., Belle Chasse LA) J. N. Darby, Hymn No. 195)

THE WORSHIP OF CAIN
HEBREWS 11:5

"By faith," we are told, "Abel offered unto God a more excellent sacrifice than Cain, by which he obtained witness that he was righteous." Thus, from the earliest dawn of human history, two ways emerged—the broad way with its wide gate, its easy road and its bitter end; and the narrow way with its one restricting gate, its hard road and its glorious end. The one begins at the gate of the garden of God and runs by way of the cross to the city of God. The other begins at the gate of the garden of Cain and runs by way of the City of Destruction to the caverns of the lost. Abel's way immediately produced a martyr. Cain's way simultaneously produced a murderer.

There are four characteristics of the worship of Cain. First, it substituted REASON FOR REVELATION. Cain and Abel both had access to the same information. It had not taken their parents long to learn that human nakedness could not be covered with the fig leaves of human effort. Sin could only be covered by the shedding of blood. An innocent substitute had to die in their stead so that a fitting covering could be theirs. Thus redeemed they stood before God, clothed at enormous cost.

Cain and Abel must often have been told these things. Hebrews 11 says it was by faith that Abel offered. Romans 10 reminds us that "faith cometh by hearing and hearing by the Word of God." So God must have made it clear and plain to both these boys that if He was to be approached at all, it must be by faith and it must be by blood. Such was the divine revelation.

76

Cain ignored the Word of God. He substituted human reasoning for Divine revelation. To his way of thinking, the way of the cross seemed monstrous. Right from the start, this liberal theologian set apart God's word and substituted his own carnal ideas.

Then, too, he substituted TRYING FOR TRUSTING. Abel would speak words such as those we find in the old hymn, "Rock of Ages":

> *"Nothing in my hand I bring,*
> *Simply to thy cross I cling;*
> *Naked look to Thee for dress,*
> *Helpless look to Thee for grace,*
> *Foul I to the fountain fly;*
> *Wash me Savior or I die."*

"Nonsense!" said Cain. Salvation has to be earned. We have to work for it, we have to suffer and earn merit. This philosophy of Cain, of course, is the very essence of all false religion. Man invented religions call upon us to fast and pray and make pilgrimages and do penance and do good works. It is the way of Cain.

Moreover, Cain substituted BEAUTY FOR BLOOD. "Without the shedding of blood," God declared, "there is no remission of sin (Heb 9:22). "When I see the blood I will pass over you," God said to Israel on the eve of their redemption (Exod. 12:13,23). Cain would have none of it. He looked at Abel's altar and he shuddered. His whole artistic soul rose up in revolt against such a "gospel of gore," as he (like modern liberal theologians) would possibly have described it. He had a better way, an aesthetically pleasing way. He planted a garden and toiled night and day. Then he built an altar of hewn stones and brought fragrant flowers and colorful fruits. He arranged them and rearranged them until he had obtained the desired effect. "Now that ought be please God," he said to his soul. It was beautiful! But it was all the fruit of the earth God had cursed and was useless as a means of salvation from sin.

Finally, he substituted PERSECUTION FOR PERSUASION. God rejected Cain's religion totally and absolutely, and Cain was furious. He went away in a rage. Then he went around and looked at Abel's altar, stained with blood, black with fire, reeking of death; and his blood boiled. Abel tried to reason with him, but a man committed to a false faith is the most unreasonable of men. Cain murdered Abel and then insolently said to God, "Am I my brother's keeper?" It was all a prelude to what the Bible calls: "The way of Cain." But that is another story.

THE WAY OF CAIN
JUDE 11

Cain went out from the presence of God a marked man, a rebel, unbowed and unrepentant. So! God had rejected his altar and his religion! Well, he would live without God. For awhile he was "a fugitive and a vagabond in the earth" (Gen. 4:12), but in time he decided to make his own way in the world. And so he did. He founded a great but godless civilization, one that was bent his way. The Holy Spirit calls it "the way of Cain." Cain organized human life and society into a way of living which left God out. The Spirit of God records a number of things about the godless way of Cain.

1. It was MATERIALISTIC. Job calls it "the old way." He tells how people told God to leave them alone while at the same time, demanding that He prove Himself to them by showing what He could do for them. As a result their houses were filled with good things and they congratulated themselves on their successes and ignored the fact that even their material prosperity really came from God (22:15-18).

2. It was HUMANISTIC. They turned their back on God. If Cain could not have his own religion, he would have no religion at all. Man could become captain of his own soul and master of his own destiny. Of the twelve people mentioned by name in the line of Cain and his descendants, only two retained any semblance of the knowledge of God—Mehujael and Methusael (Gen.4:16-24).

3. It was PROLIFIC. There was a population explosion. "Men began to multiply." This ever-increasing world population created an ever-expanding market for goods and services, especially as the antediluvian society became increasingly sophisticated.

4. It was URBANISTIC. The growing population abandoned the countryside for the city. The population became increasingly urban. God put man in a garden, Cain put him in a city and the city became an artificial paradise catering to the wants and needs of mankind.

5. It was HEDONISTIC, that is to say, it was a pleasure-driven society. The entertainment business was born, introduced by Jubal who invented music and gave people a beat to enliven their days.

6. It was PRAGMATIC. Tubal-cain brought the world through an industrial revolution and gave it a growing industry based on science, engineering and technology.

7. It was AGNOSTIC. An agnostic is a person who says you can't know, specifically, that you can't know God. This was a marked feature of Cainite civilization. It was godless (Jude 14). The Cainites ignored the testimony of Enoch and the preaching of Noah. Their minds were blinded by the god of this world. "They knew now," was the Lord's final verdict on them all. (Matt.24:39).

8 .It was DEMONIC. The human soul abhors a vacuum so those who ignore God often fall prey to evil and deceiving spirits. So it was with the Cainites who delved into the deep things of Satan and produced "a New Age" movement which, in turn, introduced strange and deadly occult phenomena. A hybrid race appeared, mirrored in later times by the fallen gods of Olympus of Greek mythology.

9. It was PORNOGRAPHIC. "Every imagination of the thoughts of men's hearts was only evil continually," the Holy Spirit says. Along with that, there was a breakdown of the primeval law of marriage. Moreover, women became prominent in Cainite society and polygamy was accepted as a lifestyle.

10. It was ANARCHISTIC. Society failed to exert restraint upon crime. Consequently, "the earth was filled with violence." The popular lifestyle was openly permissive, and everyone "did his own thing" with the nod and approval of society.

11. It was ANTAGONISTIC. The seventh from Adam in Cain's line was Lamech, an openly polygamous and a boastful murderer. This wicked man even shook his fist in the face of God and told Him to stay out of his affairs.

12. It was FATALISTIC. The idea that God might have some say about all this was ignored. Cainite society ran right through the center of a fault line where God stored up His wrath. The building of Noah's ark struck the Cainites as ludicrous. What was going to happen would happen, and there was nothing anyone could do about it. As for building an ark, that was a typical crackpot idea of the Sethites. An ark indeed!

Such was the way of Cain. In the end God destroyed that wicked society and its people. The flood came and took them all away. As God said it would.

NOAH WALKED WITH GOD
GENESIS 6:9

"Noah walked with God." The Bible tells us so. It had been a long time since God had such a close companion on earth. The last man who walked with God had been Enoch, but he had been removed by rapture seventy years before Noah was born. Right after we are told that Enoch walked with God, we are told of the birth of Noah's sons. Noah was about five hundred years old when his firstborn, Japheth was born. So it had been a long time since God had been able to find a successor to Enoch.

The world was already a wicked place, and it went on becoming worse and worse until it was totally corrupt. Every imagination of the thoughts of men's hearts was only evil continually. Moreover, the world was filled with violence (Gen.6:5).

But Noah "found grace in the eyes of the Lord." (V.8) This leads us to think of Noah as A PERSON. God said to Noah, "Thee have I found righteous" (Gen. 7:1). Noah was born in sin, just like everyone else, a child of Adam's fallen race, but there came a day when he was counted righteous by God (Rom.4:3). Righteousness is not something we acquire by doing good, it is something imparted to us by God when we believe (V.5). "Abraham believed God," we read, "and it was accounted unto him for righteousness." Something similar took place in the experience of Noah, and God wrote it into his book: "Thee have I seen righteous." God had looked into the faces of millions of men for some fifteen hundred years. He had peered into their hearts, looking for a righteous man. He only found one. His name was Noah. The name means "rest." God found Noah to be a restful person. The name also suggests "comfort." Noah had about him the characteristics of the comforter. Such was Noah as a person.

We think, also, of Noah as A PREACHER. Noah is most famous, of course, because he built the ark, a place of refuge from the wrath to come. Peter reminds us, however, that Noah was also a preacher of righteousness (2 Pet.2:8). When Paul preached righteousness to Felix, that wicked man trembled (Acts 24:25). We read of no such reaction to Noah's preaching. The people had long since become gospel hardened. Noah preached for a long time, one hundred and twenty years, and with never a convert to add to the roll. There came a day, however, when he preached for the last time. Probably his last sermon was preached at the funeral of Methuselah, whose death rang out the knell of doom over that old and evil world. Methuselah's father was the prophet Enoch. He gave his son a prophetic name: "When he dies, it shall come" was what people said when they pronounced Methuselah's name.

Finally, we think of Noah as A PARENT. Noah had no success with this world's multitudes, but he had great success with his sons. He saw them all, along with their wives, safely inside the ark. Then the door was shut, and an eerie week passed during which nothing happened. But, at last, the first great drops fell from the sky, and the waters all over the world began to rise. The ark drifted away from her cradle and out upon the rising waves, a stab of lightning pierced the gloom. Noah counted up his passengers. All was well. At least his family had believed.

May our own circle be as unbroken as his was in that day when God, once more, sends His wrath abroad. May all be in the Ark (Christ) saved from the judgment storm.

THE TEMPTATIONS OF MOSES
HEBREWS 11:24-26

Moses ranks along with Abraham, David, and Daniel as one of the truly great men of Old Testament times. His shadow lies on fifteen hundred years of Hebrew history. His influence is felt in courts of justice in the western world to this day. It all stemmed from a decision for Christ he made when he was "come to years." Satan came to him and offered him three things. First he offered him THE THRONE OF THIS WORLD. He had been found, in his little toy ark of bulrushes in the reeds along the banks of the Nile, by no less a person than the princess royal of Egypt. She had adopted him and taken him into the palace to be trained to rule. Moses was "learned in all the wisdom of the Egyptians," the Holy Spirit says. The arts and sciences, religion, and history, the art of government and the craft of war. Moses excelled in them all. And when he was a grown man, the throne itself appears to have been offered to him by the princess herself. The princess who adopted him was likely the vigorous and determined Hatshepsut, a strong willed woman, who seized the throne and reigned as sovereign in her own right. She was so strong a ruler she was able to keep Thutmose III, one of the most powerful Empire-building Pharaohs, off the throne for some twenty-two years. Doubtless Thutmose and his faction feared that Moses would supplant him.

Moses, however was controlled by his faith in God and declined the offer. He went further. He "refused to be called the son of Pharoh's daughter." Doubtless the temptor whispered: "You can use the throne to mitigate the sufferings of your fellow Hebrews in their ghetto in Goshen. You can even settle them in Canaan as allies of Egypt." Moses, however, gave up the throne of this world.

He also gave up THE THRILLS OF THIS WORLD. He turned his back on "the pleasures of sin." There was no lust he could not have indulged. There was no sin he could not have gratified, and gratified with the sly approval of the world. He "chose rather to suffer affliction with the people of God than to enjoy the pleasure of sin for a season." The Bible does not deny that there <u>are</u> pleasures in sin because, obviously, there are. The point is they do not last, nor do they satisfy. They are only "for a season."

Finally, he gave up THE THINGS OF THIS WORLD. The Egyptians were very good at making things. When Howard Carter, the Egyptologist, excavated the tomb of Tutankhamen, he found himself thirty feet from the outer door, down a long tunnel he had excavated. Before him was a second door. He made an opening in that door and thrust a candle through the opening. Lord Carnavon, his sponsor, demanded, "What is it?" "I see wonderful things," Carter finally exclaimed, "wonderful things."

Things! Wonderful things! Moses gave them all up. He "esteemed the reproach of Christ greater riches than the treasures of Egypt." So Satan left him. And God came, crowned him with glory and honor, enriched his life, and made him a renowned emancipator and legislator and an Old Testament saint as well. He will do the same for us if we make the kinds of choices Moses made.

JOCHABED

EXODUS 2:1-9

Jochabed was a Levite. So was her husband. In those days the Levites had not yet been elevated to the priestly rank, but they must have had some bent towards God, not evident in other tribes. Perhaps they were the ones who kept alive the stories and truths now written down in the book of Genesis. In any case, the Holy Spirit deems it important enough to note the fact that Amram and Jochabed were Levites.

Jochabed was the mother of Moses. The first significant fact was that SHE HAD HIM. It seems to have been a deliberate decision. She and her husband, we are told, were "not afraid of the king's commandment." The death sentence had already been signed into law—all Hebrew male children were to be thrown into the Nile—no wonder, later on, Moses turned the water of the Nile into blood. So, down there in that ghetto in Goshen, Jochabed brought to the birth a baby boy who would one day humble Egypt in the dust and change the course of history forever.

Then SHE HID HIM. The boy was born under the sentence of death. She was determined to see him soundly saved. So she began by hiding him from the world and its prince by hiding him in the haven of her home. She firmly shut the door of her house and kept out all the evil influences of the world. A godly home was her first line of defense against the world and its ways. God intends that our homes should be sanctuaries against the world and everything for which it stands. The world has its prince, motivated by a malice against the human race which beggars description. The world has its programs, and they are diametrically opposed to the Word of God. The world has its pleasures, but the Bible calls them "the pleasures of sin." Jochabed made sure that all such things were firmly shut out of her home.

But the time came, as it always does, when Moses could no longer be hidden at home. At this point, Jochabed exercised faith. She said, "How does God save those who are under the sentence of death?" She thought about Noah and his ark, and then she made a little ark for Moses. She put him in the ark and put the ark in the river. Now it was all up to God. All she could do now was watch and pray. She had now hidden him in the hollow of God's hand.

Finally, SHE HELD HIM. A series of events took place in which God demonstrated His sovereignty and His ability to defy the prince of this world. As a result Moses was adopted into the Egyptian royal family, but not until Jochabed was given the opportunity of nurturing him. Evidently she devoted her time to teaching Moses the truths which he later immortalized in the book of Genesis. Especially she drilled him in the story of Joseph (one quarter of Genesis is devoted to Joseph), the story of a young man who had lived victoriously for God in the courts of Pharoah.

Jochabed held him! No Egyptian school, no Egyptian seduction, no Egyptian sophistication had a chance. Jochabed had done her work well. She had wedded her boy to the Bible, by means of God's word, held him against all the world could offer. What a woman! Such women are desperately needed today.

As An Angel Of God

II Samuel 19:27

"My Lord the King is as an angel of God." The words were spoken by poor, broken Mephibosheth who had been maliciously slandered by Ziba, his self-seeing scoundrel of a servant. David, sad to say, more than half believed the tale that Ziba had told him, that Mephibosheth, grandson of King Saul, was planning to turn the Absalom rebellion to his own gain. But now the time had come for Mephibosheth to speak.

"YOU SOUGHT ME," he said. "You sought me!" And that was so. "Is there not yet any that is left of the house of Saul that I may show the kindness of God unto him?" David had inquired.

Ziba had told him about Mephibosheth, lame on both his feet, dwelling afar off, in virtual hiding, in hourly fear for his life. Mephibosheth had been the victim of a fall. His estates were all gone. He was living at Lo-Debar, "the place of no pasture," a dry and barren place indeed. And he had no claim on the king. His grandfather had been King Saul, a man who feared and hated David and who had tried on some two dozen occasions to murder him. So Mephibosheth was in a sorry plight. He is a prime Old Testament type of the sinner, one who has no standing before God and no claim upon Him at all.

David sought him out, however, determined to bring him back to himself. Mephibosheth remembered that.

"YOU SAVED ME," he said. "You saved me!" And so he had. David's idea just as the salvation of sinner is all God's idea, not ours. All the initiative is His.

> *"He saw me ruined by the Fall,*
> *Yet loved me notwithstanding all.*
> *He saved me from my lost estate,*
> *His lovingkindness O how great."[1]*

What must have been the feelings of Mephibosheth that day when, hobbling around the barren barnyard there in Lo-Debar, he looked up and saw horsemen on the horizon arrayed in the uniform of the palace guard.

"They've found me!" he said to himself. "They'll kill me. David has every cause to put me to death." And he plied his wretched crutches in a hopeless attempt to escape. The soldiers caught him soon enough and confronted him.

"Our lord the king," said the captain of the guard, "summons you to his presence. He wants to show you the kindness of God." Good news indeed! Grace not wrath! How like David! And how like our Lord Jesus Christ! We can be sure that Mephibosheth wasted no time in responding to the royal call.

"YOU SEATED ME," he said. "You seated me!" And so he had. For David restored all Mephibosheth's lost estates and treated him as one of the king's sons, giving him a place at his own table in Jerusalem. All this Mephibosheth remembered. He had come! He had hidden his poor, lame feet under the table of the king. Every day with David was sweeter than the day before.

And now it was his turn to speak. "My lord the king," he said, "is as an angel of God." As for Ziba and the property, let him have it all. What need did Mephibosheth have for land? He had his Lord. That was enough for him.

---

[1]Hymns of Worship and Remembrance (Belle Chase LA, Truth and Praise, Inc.) "1950, Hymn No.1 "Awake My Soul. . . ."

One Morsel Of Meat

Hebrews 12:16

"Esau, for one morsel of meat, sold his birthright." He is one of a large company, sad to say. David sold his for a short moment of passion. Judas sold his for a small margin of profit. Peter sold his at Antioch for a shallow murmur of praise. Esau sold out for a single mess of pottage. How cheaply we sell our eternal salvation or our eternal reward.

In his famous "Screwtape Letters," C. S. Lewis gives us the devil's formula for pleasure. He points out to his fellow demon, his pupil in the art of temptation, that, although pleasure has its uses as a means of seduction and enslavement, it is a tricky tool to use because it was God who invented pleasure, not Satan. The best the devil can do with pleasure is to distort it and persuade people to abuse it. They can strive to develop in them a craving for it, and get them hooked on it until they want more and more stimulation and get less and less satisfaction. The ultimate aim is to get a person's soul for nothing. Satan got Esau's cheaply enough. He got it for "one morsel of meat."

Esau and Jacob were twins. Esau was born ahead of Jacob by the narrowest of margins so, as the older brother, he stood in line to receive the patriarchal blessing. That blessing carried with it certain property rights, patriarchal rites, and priestly rights. Esau, however, cared for none of those things. Jacob did. Jacob coveted them and determined to get them at all costs, forgetful of the fact that, even before his birth, God had already promised them to him.

Esau was a man of the world. He liked to hunt and fish and sit around with the boys. He was ambitious to get on in this world. He married unsaved women and carved out a position for himself among the Dukes of Edom. He had no interest in the things of God, even though his grandfather was Abraham. Doubtless Abraham had talked to him about his conversion, how he was looking for a city which had foundations, whose builder and maker was God. It all sounded like pie in the sky by-and-by to Esau.

But not to Jacob. All his faults and failings, notwithstanding, Jacob had his priorities right. If there was one thing he wanted, it was the blessing of God in his life. He had not yet learned, however, that you cannot get spiritual things by worldly and carnal means. So Jacob set out to get Esau's birthright, no matter what it took to get it. He caught Esau when he was tired and hungry and discouraged and dangled a bowl of stew before him and clinched the deal—Esau's spiritual birthright for one serving of stew.

God never forgave Esau for his action. He called him "a profane person!" Later Esau tried to get back with a dish of venison what he had sold for a bowl of stew, but failed. He remained a profane person, a person who had no room for God, to the day of his death. That "one morsel of meat" was a costly morsel indeed. It was expensive as the "sop" Jesus handed to Judas in the upper room on the eve of His betrayal. It was a morsel that sealed his doom. For no sooner had Judas eaten it than Satan entered into him, and all hell took over his soul.

Well might we beware lest we sell our souls for a serving of this world's pleasures.

Two Big Disappointments
Genesis 12:6, 10

He had become a pilgrim and a stranger in the world in contrast with Cain who in his far-off day had become a fugitive and a vagabond on the earth.

His face was toward heaven, and his hope was in God. He was heaven-born and heaven-bound and he looked for a city whose builder and maker is God. Abraham was his name. He was a Hebrew, a migrant, one who was just passing through.

But, on the way to his home up there, he was to inherit a land down here, a promised land. And into that land, the land of Canaan he eventually came.

Imagine the shock and the dismay that were his when he discovered that there was a foe, the Canaanite, entrenched in the land. The Canaanites were a foul brood descended from Ham. They had a fierce and filthy faith. Imagine the further blow to his faith when Abraham discovered there was a famine in the land.

We know what he did. It is as plain as print on the page. He went down to Egypt and, in doing so, exchanged one set of problems for another. It was all so unnecessary, for all the time Abraham had with him all that he needed to deal with Canaanite and famine alike. He had a tent, and he had an altar. God's answer to the Canaanite was the altar; His answer to the famine was the tent. The altar was to teach him how to die to the Canaanite, the tent was to teach him how to deal with the famine.

The Canaanite represents the flesh. Often the young believer confidently expects, after his conversion, that all his problems are now solved. He expects to find nothing in his nature contrary to Christ. He is soon disappointed. The old nature is still there. More, it is awakened to active hostility to the new nature within. The believer finds he has begun what will be a war to the end. God's answer is the altar (a picture of the cross). It teaches us that "the old man," the man of old, the man we used to be (represented by the Canaanite) is crucified with Christ.

My father once asked Stephen Olford how he handled a believing brother who disliked him and sought to oppose him at every step. "Oh!"

said young Olford, "I died to him years ago." Abraham had to learn to do the same so far as the Canaanite was concerned. So do we.

But not only was the Canaanite in the land, there was also a famine in the land. The famine in the Promised Land is a picture of the world which can provide nothing to feed the spiritual nature of the believer in Christ. God's answer to the famine was a tent. Abraham lived in a tent, not a house. The tent was there to remind Abraham that he had already judged and forsaken this world. He was not to expect anything from this world which is a barren place for the child of God. He was to strike his tent and move on as God led the way (Heb.11:8-10; 15-16). He was to keep his eye on heaven, his final and eternal home. In the meantime he could well have sung:

> "I am a stranger here
> Within a foreign land,
> My home is far away
> Upon a golden strand."

In the end, after his disastrous Egyptian venture, Abraham had to come back to the place where his tent and altar had been at the beginning. That is how it always is for all those who have become pilgrims and strangers down here, citizens of a better land over there.

MOUNT MORIAH
GENESIS 22

Mt. Moriah! From the first time he heard of the place, it haunted Abraham's dreams and turned them into nightmares. The name means "Foreseen by Jehovah."

Sir Edmund Hilliary reached the summit of Mount Everest on May 9, 1953. At 29,002 feet above sea level, he stood at the top of the world, thanks to team work, good equipment and cooperating weather. But Everest is dwarfed by Mount Moriah just as Mount Moriah is dwarfed by

Mount Calvary. Mount Moriah, after all, represents only one of the pictorial shadows cast by Calvary. But even the shadow has a great deal to say.

We think, first, of THE SUPREME TEST. The story begins and ends with the same words: "And it came to pass after these things" (22:1). For Calvary was the <u>consummation</u> of a plan, thought out in eternity, to bring salvation to mankind. Many things led up to the death of Christ on that cruel Roman cross, on that skull-shaped hill, in that ancient city of Jerusalem, famous for stoning its saints and slaughtering its seers.

"And it came to pass after these things" (22:20). For Calvary was the <u>commencement</u> of a plan, thought out in eternity, to bring in a Church. The story of Mount Moriah in Genesis 22 only prepares us for the call of Rebekah in Genesis 24 just as the mystery of the cross prepares us for the mystery of the Church. All was foreseen of Jehovah, but Abraham did not yet know that.

Out of the blue, came the terrible test: "Take now thy son, thine only son Isaac, whom thou lovest, and get thee into the land of Moriah and offer him up there . . ." All Abraham's love, all his hopes, all the future of his race rested in Isaac. And all his joy and laugher and all of his plans and purposes were centered in his son. Must it all end abruptly in blood and flame? What a test!

We think not only of the supreme TEST, we think also of THE SUPREME TRUST. Abraham had God's word for it: "<u>In Isaac</u> shall thy seed be called." Would his trust reach beyond the tomb and the death of all his hopes? Hebrews 11 says that it did. For Abraham dared to believe that if he offered up Isaac, God would raise him back to life. That was sublime faith which enabled him to say to his servants: "Stay here. I and the lad will go yonder and worship <u>and come again</u> to you here."

So the wood, a burden borne by others up to now was thrust upon Isaac. More! Isaac could see the knife (speaking of death), and the fire (speaking of that which comes after death). Yet in perfect love, obedience and confidence in his father, he went with him to the dreaded Mount. "Both of them together!" "Both of them together!" The Holy Spirit writes it down twice. Isaac was not dragged fighting and protesting to the hill of death. As with Christ, who went willingly to Calvary, so with Isaac. He and the father were in this thing together.

Which brings us to THE SUPREME TRUTH. The whole story is obviously a type. A lamb would be provided. That is the supreme truth this story tells. God said, in effect, to Abraham: "I want you as a human father to take your only begotten son to a place called Mt. Moriah, a place foreseen by Jehovah, and I want you to offer him up there as a burnt offering so that the world may know what it will cost me, as a Heavenly Father, to take my only begotten Son to a place called Mount Calvary and offer him up there as an atonement for all mankind. For that, too, was "foreseen by Jehovah." More! It was foreseen by Jehovah that there would be no ram caught by its horns and spare God's own dear Son when His time came. As Abraham watched the flames ascend, to consume the sacrifice God had provided, how he would have appreciated the words of this great hymn of the church:

> *"When I think that God His Son not sparing,*
> *Sent Him to die, I scarce can take it in,*
> *That on the cross, my burdens gladly bearing,*
> *He bled and died to take away my sin."*

THE DEATH OF SARAH
GENESIS 23:1-19

Genesis is a book of funerals. The angel of death, the grim reaper, haunts it from beginning to end. The first death was a murder, but it also made a martyr. The last death was that of a rich and powerful man, dying in his bed, surrounded by his loved ones and placed in a coffin worth a king's ransom. But Joseph in his coffin was just as dead as poor Abel, his stabbed and bludgeoned body left to rot by the way to his house.

But of all the numerous deaths recorded in Genesis, there is none so sad as this one, sandwiched between a chapter which portrays the mystery of Christ's cross (Gen. 22) and a chapter which portrays the mystery of Christ's church (Gen. 24). The death of Sarah, between these two peaks, portrays the setting aside of Israel for this present age. Though Abraham, of course, could have known nothing of such truths, truths not to be revealed for another two thousand years.

We begin with ABRAHAM'S GRIEF. His beloved Sarah was 127 years old (she is the only woman in the Bible whose age is recorded), but she looked more like twenty-seven. Kings had lusted after her beauty even in her old age. Her death left Abraham empty. Her name means "princess"; and, like one born to rule, she was forever enthroned on the empire of Abraham's heart.

No longer would Sarah's bewitching smile bring sunshine to his soul. No longer would her imperious voice be heard in the servant's tents. No longer would she and Abraham sit together in the cool of the day talking together, praying together, content to be together. Abraham sat now alone in his princely tent, his thoughts full of that city which hath foundations, whose builder and maker is God. That heavenly Jerusalem was doubly dear to him now for God, his Friend, was there and Sarah, his wife, was there. He wished that he, too, was there.

We think, next of SARAH'S GRAVE. Her soul was in heaven, but her mortal clay needed a tomb so Abraham appealed to members of a nearby Canaanite clan, to the sons of Heth. Controlling his tears, he said: "I am a stranger and sojourner among you. Provide me a place for a tomb." Ever since Abraham's astounding victory over the kings of the east (Gen.14), the people of Canaan prudently held him in awe. "Thou art a mighty prince among us," they said. After this exchange of pleasantries, serious negotiations began. Abraham wanted a tomb; and Ephron, who had a suitable site for sale, wanted cold cash. No doubt Ephron set a ridiculously high price for the land as he expected Abraham to haggle, but price was no issue with Abraham. He was rich.

The story closes with EPHRON'S GIFT. When Abraham indicated what piece of property he desired, the sheik said: I give it to you, my lord," but he would have been astonished and outraged if Abraham had taken him up on his words. That was but the opening gambit in an enjoyable bout of bargaining. "How much?" said Abraham. Ephron, expecting considerable hot debate, fixed the price at four hundred shekels and was doubtless astonished when Abraham paid him his price. The deed was "made sure" to Abraham. How sure? All we know is that Jacob had to pay for it again later on.

Such was Ephron's "gift." Not as the world giveth give I unto you,"
Jesus says to us. His promise is sure (Rom4:16), the Holy Spirit declares.
How thankful we are that God's gift of eternal life is made sure in His son
and that our title deeds to glory are as safe as God's throne.

HOSEA

HOSEA 1:1-11

A century and a half had come and gone since Jeroboam I had torn ten of
the tribes away from the throne of David. Some fourteen kings had come
and gone. Some had been weak, some had been warlike and all had been
wicked. Jeroboam had set the trend. He introduced the cult of the golden
calf. It was a bad beginning. Later on Ahab had introduced Jezebel, the
false worship of Baal and the filthy worship of Ashtoreth. Now Jeroboam
II was on the throne and, though outwardly strong, he had been weighed in
the balance and found wanting, so God sent along a prophet, Hosea by
name. His task was to show the king, the court and the country just what
God thought of them all.

The prophet had a TRAGEDY IN HIS HOMELIFE. It was a full-
length portrait of the TRAGEDY IN HIS HOMELAND. A look at what
Hosea's homelife was like tells us all we need to know as to what his
homeland was like. Hosea had no illusions regarding the state of his homeland. It was apostate.

As a young preacher, Hosea felt the need for a wife, someone to support
him and to share with him in what he was sure would be a difficult ministry.
The Spirit of God confirmed his leading and, shortly afterwards, he met
Gomer. Probably the kind of wife Hosea envisioned for himself was someone
like Sarah or Miriam or Jochabed, or Deborah, some strong believer in God.

But his choice was Gomer. It seemed a good enough choice for her
name meant "completion." He thought she would be a true help meet. She
would complete him, bringing strength where he felt weakness, goodness
where he was inclined to stray. "Completion." So Gomer won his heart,
and God confirmed to him that she was the one he should marry. What a

shock he received! "A wife of whoredoms" is the Holy Spirit's later assessment of her. She was a woman given to a promiscuous lifestyle.

Whether Hosea knew it or not, we cannot be sure. If he did, doubtless he deluded himself into thinking he would change her. After all Rahab been a harlot but became a true mother in Israel and a giant of the faith. Instead, Gomer broke Hosea's heart.

That was the supreme truth he was to show to Israel. He became a man of sorrows, acquainted with grief. He was married to a wife of whoredoms. Painfully he learned that sin not only breaks God's laws; it breaks God's heart. So Hosea married Gomer. The tragedy in his homelife had begun.

A boy was born, and the prophet called him Jezreel. The name means "vengeance." It was the name of a place of fearful associations. Naboth's vineyard had been there. The battle of Armageddon will be fought there.

But by now, Gomer was tired of a restraint, and Hosea had to put up with her moods. In time, a second child was born. Hosea had grave doubts as to its parentage so he called it "Lo-Ruhamah". The name means "she who never knew a father's love." Then Gomer became a woman of the streets, and Hosea disowned her third child altogether. "Lo-Ammi" he called it—"no child of mine." The names of these children were prophetic messages addressed to apostate Israel. They warned of vengeance, of being strangers to God and of being disowned by Him.

Gomer sank deeper and deeper into the mire until she gave herself up totally to vice. Then she became a drunkard and sold herself to prostitution. Hosea loved her still. In the end, he bought her from her owner for a few pennies—all she was worth, and took her to his home. He cleaned her up and gave her a bed. "I've bought you," he told her. "I still love you. But I don't want a slave. It's a wife that I want. I know how to wait."

Thus God loved Israel, and thus He loves the world. "Love suffers long and is kind," He says. His love never lets us go. It pursues us even into the far country. "His love knows no limit to its endurance, no end to its trust," as one translator puts it. It never fails.

JOEL
JOEL 1:15

Joel looms up out of nowhere, raises his voice, then vanishes back into the shadows. He seems to have been the very first of the writing prophets. He wrote six dozen verses, that's all. But for all that, this so-called <u>minor</u> prophet was the herald of a <u>major</u> departure in the prophetic world. Joel wrote things down.

Shakespeare makes the envious Cassius say about Julius Caesar: "Why man, he doth bestride the world like a colossus." The same could have been said of Joel.

Two days occupied Joel. Just two days. The first was THE DAY OF THE LOCUST. There had been rumours in Israel of a brewing plague in the southeastern deserts of the Middle East. Then, one day the sky turned black; and the locusts arrived. They descended by the millions on farm and field and forest. They covered the ground to a depth of one and a half feet. They ate every stalk and every stem, every leaf and every twig. "Incarnate hunger!" best describes what they were. When at last they moved on, they left utter devastation in their wake. It was a divine visitation, herald of worse ones to come.

Then there was THE DAY OF THE LORD. Half a dozen prophets talk about this day, but it was Joel who mentioned it first. Four concepts whirled in Joel's mind as he thought of this great judgment to come.

First, there were <u>fading voices</u>. It was only a matter of decades from Elijah and Elisha to Joel. These two men, armed with might and miracle, had been a nine-day wonder in Israel. People remembered their miracles; but a few remembered their message. Joel saw the need to write things down, to give people something more important than miracles, to give them a book.

The comfortable little Palestinian world was changing, and the age of the super powers had arrived. The hostile neighboring countries of Moab and Edom and the like were nothing compared with Assyria, Babylon, Greece, and Rome. Joel saw it coming on the wings of the wind, the destruction, the desolation and the deportation, all the inevitable fruit of apostasy. God's people would need something to hold on to. So, where Elijah produced miracles, Joel produced a manuscript.

Then there were <u>former values</u>. God had planned for Israel to be located on the crossroads of continents so that they might be a testimony to all mankind, the world's schoolmaster to bring people from many nations to Christ. A century of liberal theology, however, had rendered Israel apostate and impotent. The old landmarks had been removed, the old faith had been replaced, the old values had been erased. It called for judgment.

So now the nation faced <u>fearful vengeance</u>. Had Israel remained true to its call, these gentile superpowers would have come; but they would have come, not as warriors, but as worshippers. Before it was too late, Israel must repent. It was still not too late in Joel's day, but it was "repent—or else!"

But Joel still had some good news. There were to be <u>future visitations</u> for his most important prophecy had to do with an outpouring of the Holy Spirit. It took eight hundred years for Joel's prophecy of Pentecost to be fulfilled. But the outpouring did come, and we are living in the reality of it to this day. "Thank you, Joel. There was nothing <u>minor</u> about you!"

AMOS

AMOS 3:3

In the days of Amos, both Israel and Judah appeared to be prosperous. Jeroboam II ruled Israel; and King Uzziah, one of Judah's handful of godly kings, reigned in power. But it was all deceptive. Corruption and decay had advanced to the point in Israel where there was no remedy. Judgment was inevitable. Temporary revivals in Judea would postpone that country's fall, but the rot had already gone too deep in Israel.

When <u>revival</u> is no longer an option, God sends <u>ruin</u>. Already, over the distant northern skyline, the Assyrian army was preparing to march. Its arrival would bring vengeance, and Amos knew it to be so. For centuries Israel and Judah had been made up of fighting farmers. There had been a rural economy and life-style. Life had been generally simple and wholesome. But now society had become urbanized, sophisticated and worldly-wise. It was a situation which heralded judgment to come. Amos himself was a farmer. He was also very poor. He was what we would call a cowboy or a herdsman. His hometown was perched on the edge of a fearful desert. What he saw of urban society shocked and outraged him. We can imagine the effect he had on high society in sophisticated Samaria when he came clomping into the halls of polite people in his cowboy boots and when he addressed the cultured court women as "Ye kine of Bashan, you barnyard cows!"

We suspect that, nevertheless, he was received, at first, with some enthusiasm in Israel for he began by denouncing the surrounding city-states of Damascus, Gaza, Tyre, Edom, Ammon, Moab, and even Judah. But when he turned on Israel, it was a different story. The Israelites were furious.

By the time his scathing tongue lashed out at them, the Israelites recognized his formula—"For three transgressions and for four. . ." It expressed a Hebrew idiom. It means that the cup of God's wrath was not only full, it was more than full.

Amos was fond of using illustrations, usually drawn from desolate desert scenes familiar to him since boyhood days. For instance, he remembered once seeing a shepherd saving, from the maw of a glutted lion, all that was left of a sheep—a pair of shin bones and the tattered fragment of an ear. That was all. And that was what Israel could look forward to, when the Assyrians would be finished with them.

He pictures, also, a city after the army of Assyria had ravished it. He describes a house of ten family members with only one sole survivor. He sees that wretched man, ravished by the plague, cowering in some dark corner. A relative comes to burn the bodies of the dead; but he hovers outside, afraid to go in lest he, too, catch the plague. He calls. The sole survivor is terrified. He is afraid that the echoing voice will precipitate some new horror. "Hush!" he says. "Be quiet."

Like Joel and others, Amos saw the day of the Lord and pictures the terror of end-time events. He sees a man fleeing from a lion, only to run into the arms of a bear. He pictures a fleeing man leaning, exhausted, against a wall, only to be bitten by a serpent. He sees a man praying; but, alas, he does not know God and the Bible is, to him, an unknown book. How can he pray?

All this was the end result of the calf cult which had slowly poisoned the whole Northern Kingdom. It had been founded on a wholesale application of Bible-twisting, liberal theology. No wonder that the sight of the golden calf in Bethel gave wings to the prophet's words. So, where Hosea preached <u>love</u>, Amos preached <u>law</u>. While Hosea was full of feeling, Amos was full of facts. Where Hosea went into his house for his illustrations, Amos scoured the nations and the wilds.

If God were to send a modern cowboy to stalk the halls of Congress and the White House with a message for America, what would he say? He would probably simply preach what Amos preached—wrath! Wrath already on the way.

MICAH

MICAH 7:18

"Who is like Jehovah?" That is what this man's name means. Evidently Micah's father wanted to make sure that Micah never forgot that truth. He was reminded of it every time he heard or wrote his name—"WHO is like JEHOVAH?" The answer obviously was no one! Especially the false gods of the heathen.

He came from Mareshah, a town on the Philistine border and, therefore, constantly threatened by those ancient foes of Israel. And that is all we know about this man, just his name and his address, and the fact that he was a prophet, and also the words that he spoke.

We can sense his reaction when God called him: "Me? Why do you want <u>me</u>? After all, you've got Isaiah, and he's a very big prophet indeed. Moreover he is cousin to the king, he has friends in high places, he is eloquent in the scriptures and he has a tremendous grasp of current events." Why do you want me? The answer was, of course, that the Old Testament law required a two-fold witness before truth could be established.

Already the shadow of Assyria lay over the land of the Hebrew people. Weak King Ahaz of Judah, alarmed by the Syro-Ephraimitic alliance of Syria and Israel against him, and disdainful of Isaiah's warnings, had appealed to Assyria for help. It was a foolish thing to do, like inviting the cat into the cage to keep peace between the canaries.

But if the Assyrian was coming, so was God. His feet would soon be "trampling out the vintage where the grapes of wrath were stored." The worship of Baal, the nature god, of foul Ashtaroth and of fierce Moloch had taken over the land. God was coming in wrath. The earth had already begun to shake beneath His feet. Volcanoes erupted. The stones cried out. And dark was His path on the wings of the storm.

Samaria was the swirling vortex towards which the energy of the approaching storm was directed. Beautiful Samaria, drowning in the vileness, the violence and vanity of its false and futile faiths. Its massive temple of Baal had been paid for by the hire of her harlot priestesses.

Worse still, all this religious infamy had now been imported into Judah. Nor could godly King Hezekiah, nor the great and gifted prophet, Isaiah, stem the rising tide of wickedness in the land.

Even while Micah was preaching, weak King Ahaz, father of Hezekiah, was busy importing a pagan altar from Damascus. Solomon's great brazen altar was to be pushed out of the way and this heathen altar installed in its place.

No wonder the Assyrian was coming. The prophet made puns of the place names, places in the path of the coming conqueror, puns such as: Rolling-in-the-dust-at-Dust-Town; Falsehoods-paid-for-at-False-Town; and so on. There was, however, another town that told a better tale and Micah is the one who put that town forever on the map. The town was Bethlehem! There, in that little backwoods Judean town, the Christ of God would one day enter into human life. Micah said so.

Then Micah remembered an unrecorded and almost forgotten fragment of an old Bible tale. It was the story of Balaam, the Mesopotamian psychic and of his wily employer, King Balak of Moab. Moses had told the tale of Balaam and his sins, his sermons and his final suggestion. But Micah remembered another sermon this pagan prophet preached. "What would God take as fair payment for my sins?" the King of Moab asked. Then, like a man haggling in the market place, he kept on raising his price. Finally, he reached his limit. He would give his firstborn son on the altar of sacrifice, the fruit of his body, for the sin of his soul. "If you wish to buy your salvation, my Lord King," the prophet had replied, "then do justly, love mercy and walk humbly before God." But it was too late for Israel. Judgment was on the way.

Micah makes one more pun before he puts down his pen, a pun, indeed, on his very own name: "Who is like unto God?, God who delighteth in mercy?" It was the rainbows shining forth on the wings of the storm. The promise of grace in the midst of wrath to come.

NAHUM

NAHUM 1:1-3

In the year 664 B.C. the great Egyptian city of Thebes fell to the Assyrians. It was a great triumph for Assyrian arms. Indeed it seemed as though there would be no end to Assyria's nightmare victories. But an unknown Hebrew prophet, Nahum by name, felt the fire of divine inspiration burn in his soul. "Yet fifty years and Assyria would be overthrown!" That was his cry.

He saw it all. He saw the gradual formation of a coalition of gentile nations who had long plotted vengeance on Assyria. He saw the mobilization of allied armies united now against the common foe. He saw the collapse of Assyria's outposts and the withdrawal of the Assyrians behind the walls of Nineveh. He saw the strategies of the allied forces. And then, oh joy!, he saw the sudden, catastrophic, chaotic crash of the cruelest empire the world had ever known. Nahum saw it all. Nearly a hundred years before, Jonah had preached just such an overthrow to the great Assyrian city of Nineveh but the judgment had been stayed by repentance. How Jonah would have envied Nahum! For now the time for mercy was past. Assyria had crossed that fateful boundary line God draws around such wicked empires, and its doom was sealed.

The roll call of Assyria's kings was the roll call of cruelty and carnage. There was Shalmaneser III, who called himself, "The Mighty King," and Tiglath-Pilesar III, who turned Assyria into a superpower. There was Shalmaneser V, who invaded Israel and lay siege to Samaria, and Sargon II, who put an end to Israel and deported ten of the tribes. There was Sennacherib, who was fiendishly cruel and who invaded Judah, and whose army God smote before the gates of Jerusalem. There was Esarhaddon, who carried victorious Assyrian arms into Egypt and who humbled wicked King Manasseh in the dust. There was Ashurbanipal, who captured Thebes and who stirred Nahum's soul so that, set on fire by God, he proclaimed the utter ruin of Assyria fifty years before the event, and at a time when the evil empire seemed all victorious. It was a long and dark, blood-soaked, terrifying chapter of history that the Assyrians left behind.

There was no end to the horrors. Captured nobles were flayed alive. Captives were burned. Prisoners of war were impaled on stakes. And it had gone on and on for some six hundred years. No wonder Nahum named Nineveh "that bloody city." No wonder, too, that a vast and heartfelt sigh of relief went up from all the surrounding countries when the news finally came—Nineveh was no more! Never again would Assyria's dreaded storm troops march out of Nineveh's gates to torment the cities of men.

"The Lord is slow to anger," said Nahum. Nineveh itself was proof of that. :The Lord is slow to anger, and great in power, and will not acquit the guilty." He added some further words. Nineveh was to be, "empty and void and waste."

The sun of Nineveh sank swiftly when the time came. Within fifty years of its fall, all the commerce of the world, which had beaten a path to its door, fell back into its old, familiar routes. And Nineveh was lost to history and its very location but a vague memory.

Nahum teaches us that "the mills of God grind slowly but they grind exceeding small." As Nebuchadnezzar learned: "The heavens do rule."

OBADIAH

Obadiah's book is little more than a mere pamphlet. Indeed, it contains less than two dozen words. It is, in fact, a tale of two cities, Petra and Jerusalem. It is also the story of two peoples, the Edomites and the Jews. Moreover, it is the story of twins, Esau and Jacob—unidentical twins, different in appearance, different in appetite, different in appeal. The one boy, Esau, appealed to his father. The other boy, Jacob, appealed to his mother. The one boy was a killer, a wild man, a professional hunter. The other boy was a keeper, one who had a heart for the flock.

From these two boys came two nations. The nation of Edom, which descended from Esau, was wild, godless and proud, living on the plunder of caravans and of wayfaring men. The other nation, Israel, descended from Jacob, was a chosen nation, raised up by God to be a testimony to all others. There was a long history of war and strife between these two peoples. Had the Edomites held out a helping hand to the Hebrews, on their way from Egypt to Canaan, the story might have been a different one. The Edomites might have found shelter beneath the wings of Jehovah. Instead they chose rather to hinder and oppose. In the end they produced a man called Herod the Great, the monster of a man who tried to murder the infant Christ of God in His bed.

The most spectacular city of Edom was the rock city of Petra. It was surrounded by a wild, untamed terrain, a tangle of mountains, deep canyons, rock shelves with here and there strips of fertile land. Here was the haunt of the sliding serpent, the stinging scorpion, the soaring eagle. The Edomites thought their country to be impregnable and boasted of their place in the sun.

When Nebuchadnezzar invaded Jerusalem, the Edomites were thrilled. They became his willing aides, following in the wake of the Babylonian conquerors, urging them on, cheering their triumphs, helping them round up fleeing Jews. When Jerusalem fell, they cheered and fell on the spoil. Moreover, they took an active part in sacking the city, catching fleeing Jews, and in seizing their land.

No wonder Obadiah spoke out: "Though thou exalt thyself as the eagle, and though thou set thy nest among the stars, I will bring thee down," saith the Lord. "Thou shalt be cut off forever." And so it came to be. The rock city of Petra is now just a place for tourists to go.

As for that other city, Jerusalem, the prophet had a word for her, too. Ruin for Petra! Restoration for Judah! And that, too, has come to be. Yea, and beyond the turmoil of today, in the coming Day of the Lord, the prophet saw a triumphant Zion. He saw the banners of the Christ unfurled and the nations trooping to Jerusalem proclaiming, "Holiness to the Lord."

Obadiah teaches us that God is ever on the throne. In the end, He always settles accounts with those who attack His own. More, God does not allow a temporary lapse by His people, however sad and serious it may be, to turn Him from His goals—whether for Israel or for His Church.

JONAH

Down! Down! Down! Thus the Holy Spirit describes Jonah's early steps in his life of disobedience. Moreover, it was not until he touched bottom that this Old Testament prodigal came to himself.

First, we have THE WORD FROM GOD. "The word of the Lord came unto Jonah." Jonah had no doubt as to either the source or the substance of the word that came to him: "Arise, go to Nineveh that great city and cry against it for their wickedness is come up before me." What galled Jonah was the knowledge that, if he did as he was told, Nineveh might repent. And if Nineveh repented, then God would change his mind; and Nineveh would be spared—to become the very rod of God to thrash guilty Israel. Jonah decided that Nineveh was the last place he intended to go.

So he took off for Tarshish, to what in those days was "the uttermost part of the earth." "Yet forty days and Nineveh shall be overthrown." That was the message. Well, it would take God more than forty days to catch up to him!

Then came THE WORD WITH GOD. For God had both the wind and the whale waiting for this willful prophet. He would give this wayward witness of His a taste of that hell to which he was all too ready to consign the Ninevites. Indeed, that is just where Jonah eventually confessed himself to be—in "the belly of hell." He endured his terrors for three days and three nights before he was willing to go to Nineveh. God had no thought of changing His mind. So, finally, Jonah prayed, oh, how he prayed! Verse after verse of the Psalms came to mind. He strung them together in a string of pleas for help. And God heard and answered, and the word came to him again: "Yet forty days and Nineveh shall be overthrown." Jonah discovered that the sandglass of forty days was set to run, not from the time he received the message, but from the time Nineveh did.

So comes THE WORD FOR GOD. He went to Nineveh and, arriving at its gate, he must have been a ghastly sight. The gastric juices of the whale had doubtless done their deadly work. He looked like a living corpse. He began to preach. His prophecy contained only eight words: "Yet forty days and Nineveh shall be overthrown," but Jonah preached them with authority and power. He, himself, was the real message, a living epistle to be known and read of all men. The terrified Ninevites looked at Jonah, listened to Jonah and repented to the last man, woman and child.

And Jonah sulked. He sat in his shanty at a spot where he could see the fires fall. And nothing happened. He was enraged. He complained bitterly to God. And God stooped down to reason with him. The last we see of Jonah he was still sulking, still mad, like the elder brother of the Lord's parable (Lk.15:25-32). But, in the end, he too repented. He went home and wrote his book. And God put it in the Bible. And Jonah has rejoiced ever since, with joy unspeakable and full of glory, as people in all ages and in many lands have read his book and been saved, or studied it and responded to the call to proclaim God's word in all parts of the world.

ZEPHANIAH
ZEPHANIAH 1:14-16

His name means "Hidden by Jehovah." We must never forget we live on a conquered planet, that its prince and god is fallen Lucifer and that he nurses, in the deep, dark dungeons of his being, an implacable hatred for God and for His people. It is not unusual for God's people to have to be hidden. Moses was hidden by his mother. Elijah was hidden by God. Jesus was hidden. Of the thirty-three-and-a-half years He lived on earth, thirty of them were hidden years.

Zephaniah was hidden. He had a secret; and it was, of necessity, a closely guarded secret. He was a great grandson of godly King Hezekiah. During the long reign of wicked King Manasseh, it would have been as good as a death warrant to let a secret like that be known. Now that good King Josiah was on the throne, seeking to undo the damage Manasseh and Amnon had done, it had suddenly become an asset to be related to the throne. So, after hiding this family secret for three generations now, in the fourth generation it could be made known. And that is how Zephaniah begins. He proclaims his royal lineage.

The HIDING gives place to the HAUNTING. There was a ghost, a grim and ghastly one at that, which haunted the prophet Zephaniah. He had another secret, and it was one which could not be hidden. What haunted Zephaniah was <u>his</u> particular vision of "The day of the Lord." That day, first injected into the prophetic picture by Joel, is mentioned twenty times in the Old Testament and four times in the New. Half a dozen prophets had a hand in describing it, including the great prophet Isaiah. But it was Zephaniah who clearly saw that the Day of the Lord was to be equated with the end times. He calls it "the day of the Lord's anger." A day when <u>war</u>, <u>weather</u>, and <u>woe</u> combine to shake this planet to its core.

And suddenly there was HORROR. For coming back to the present, from one of his excursions into the far future, Zephaniah saw something else which struck terror to his soul. All about him was evidence of the damage done to the nation by Manasseh, damage good King Josiah could never hope to repair. Then Zephaniah saw it. He cried out. "<u>The LORD is in the midst!</u>" he declared. The living God had come in person to collect fuel for the fire of His wrath and what He saw determined Him. He would cut good King Josiah short, in his prime and remove Judah's last hope of salvation. Then He wrote "bankrupt" over Judah's account and sealed its doom.

But even so there was HOPE. The prophet realized, at last, that there was another side to things. The "day of the Lord" did not just terminate at Meggido in chaos and carnage. It carried on to the <u>Golden Age</u> of the millennial age.

So, at last, there was HAPPINESS. "Sing!" he cried. "Shout! Be glad! Rejoice!"

> *"Dark, dark will be the midnight*
> *But dayspring is at hand*
> *And glory, glory dwelleth*
> *In Emmanuel's land."*

HABAKKUK

HABAKKUK 3:18-19

Habakkuk looms up in the darkness which covered the land of Judah when wicked King Manasseh sat upon the throne. He looks about him. He lodges a bitter complaint at the Supreme Court of heaven. He listens in astonishment to the answer he gets. He looks about him some more. He laughs suddenly, then vanishes back into the shadows, leaving us with one great truth: The just shall live by faith.

In actual fact, Habakkuk seems to have been more concerned about solving a problem than in delivering a prophecy. We note THE SILENCE OF GOD WHICH CAUSED HIS PROBLEM. It is a problem as old as man. Why does God remain silent when wickedness seems to be triumphant everywhere?

Manasseh, the son of godly King Hazekiah, was the longest reigning and wickedest of all the Judean kings. The nation never recovered from his apostasies. The calf cult was given full and free reign. The worship of Baal was supported by the throne. The Assyrian and Chaldee worship of the sun, the moon, and the stars was in vogue, along with a full fledged belief in astrology. Sodomy was an alternate lifestyle, its perverts being given honored place near the temple. And there, in the temple court itself, was the Asherah, towering up like a beacon, a shameless sex object, glorifying lust. And, worst of all, the terrible worship of Moloch had the king's complete support. Such was Manasseh's Jerusalem.

And God was silent. No wonder Habakkuk was perplexed, especially as all this moral and spiritual collapse had come swiftly on the heels of Hezekiah's great reforms. Which brings us to THE STATEMENT OF GOD WHICH COMPOUNDED HIS PROBLEM. "

"Don't worry!" God said to his puzzled prophet. "I have already prepared my answer to your problem. I am going to hand Judah over to the Babylonians!" Habakkuk was more horrified than ever. The cure was worse than the complaint. Judah was sinful, for sure—but the Babylonians were a thousand times worse. The solution made no sense at all. Which, in turn, brings us to THE SOVEREIGNTY OF GOD WHICH CANCELED THE PROBLEM.

God told his servant that He knew all about the Babylonians. He knew about their greed, their goals, their guilt, their guile and their gods. "Don't worry about the Babylonians," He declared, "their doom is only a matter of time."

The prophet was taught that when contemplating the equation of God's dealings with the human race, he must always take two factors into consideration. First there was the <u>time</u> factor. God's calendar is far bigger than ours. He is always on time.

Then, too he must take into account, the <u>trust</u> factor. "Trust Me," God said, "the just shall live by FAITH." So much for the <u>Babylonian</u> issue.

But now for the <u>broader</u> issue. God enlarged the vision of his servant and gave him a glimpse of end-time events, events which far eclipsed the events of his own day. And suddenly, Habakkuk broke into song.

"The just shall live by faith." As the truth of it got hold of the prophet, it put a spring into his step and a song into his soul. It will do the same for us.

HAGGAI

Haggai was a very old man. As a boy he had been hauled off to Babylon as a slave. Behind him lay the smoking ruins of Jerusalem and the Temple. Alongside him tramped the surviving remnant of the chosen people of God.

At length the boy captive saw the city itself, great Babylon which sat astride the Euphrates and ruled the world. It was to be his home from boyhood to old age. But he would never forget his roots. He would recall a thousand times the promises of Jeremiah and the preaching of Ezekiel. The startling visions of Daniel also would come to mind, visions which ran down the avenues of time to distant ages yet unborn.

His generation grew up, and another took its place. Haggai could not help but notice that this new generation had little longing left for the land of promise which had so stirred his own heart. Indeed, when Cyrus issued his famous decree, emancipating the Jewish captives he had inherited from the Babylonians, most Jews weren't interested at all. They had been born in Babylon. They had made it their home. The vast Persian Empire, covering some two million square miles, was their Emporium. It was a great place to do business and grow rich. Of the twenty-four orders of priests, only four took Cyrus seriously. Of the entire Levitical tribe, only seventy-four responded. The treasures and pleasures of Babylon had most of the Jews in their grip.

Haggai, however, responded with joy. He was going home! And, at first, his hopes burned high for when they arrived back in Jerusalem an altar was built, and the foundations of a new temple were laid. But then it all fizzled out, and Haggai was outraged. The Spirit of God fell upon him, and He began to preach.

"Consider your ways," he cried, "consider your ways." They were eating and drinking, buying and building, plowing and planting—and God blew on it, and it all came to nothing. Why? Because God's house was being neglected—that was why.

When finally, under the lash and spur of Haggai, the people finally stirred themselves and completed the house, another problem surfaced. The old men wept because they remembered the glittering, golden splendor of Solomon's Temple and this new temple was a mere ghost of a temple compared with that one. They wept. "Never mind!" God said, "This house will be blessed in a way never known by Solomon's Temple. God Himself will visit this temple. And so it was that when Jesus came, He did indeed visit that temple. He visited it as a Babe in Mary's arms, as a Boy full grown and as a Man, whip in hand and with fire in His eye, come to cast out and cleanse. Solomon's golden shrine had watched in vain for such a visitation of God manifest in flesh.

The bottom line, as we would say, in Haggai's prophecy, was simply this—If we put God's house first, God will put our house first.

ZECHARIAH

Haggai and Zechariah were contemporaries. Haggai was an old man, Zechariah was a young one. The Lord referred to him in his denunciation of Jerusalem: "Ye serpents, ye generation of vipers, how can ye escape the damnation of hell? upon you shall come all the righteous blood shed upon the earth from the blood of righteous Abel unto the blood of Zacharias, the son of Barachias, whom ye slew between the temple and the altar" (Matt.23:33-35). Abel was the first martyr in the Old Testament, and the prophet Zechariah was the last.

The temple had been finished, thanks to the spur and lash of old Haggai. But the Canaanite was now in the house of the Lord. Zechariah was outraged. At first, his prophecies took an apocalyptic turn, he looked far down the distant ages and his preaching was far beyond the grasp of his hearers.

"I see a red horse!" he cried. "Now I see four horns and four carpenters." He might as well have been speaking a foreign language. "I see a man measuring the city! I can see the high priest in filthy raiment! Now I see a Branch, now two olive trees, Now I see an enormous flying scroll. Now I see a woman sitting in a container. Now come two women with wide wings like a stork. They are carrying the woman to Babylon. Now I see four chariots and multi-colored horses going off in all directions. And now, mark this well, I see the high priest being crowned like a king."

We can well imagine Zechariah's fellows made no sense at all of all that. Indeed, to this very day, multitudes in the church still cannot decode the apocalyptic message Zechariah gave. We can well imagine that, to say the least, the Jews were increasingly annoyed with the prophet for setting forth truth they simply could not grasp.

Not that they liked him any better when he put aside his riddles and spoke in plain language.

He foretold both the coming Greek and Roman invasions, and both the first and second comings of Christ. He saw Jesus riding in triumph into Jerusalem—on a donkey of all things. He saw the coming of the Antichrist. He saw Christ being sold for a handful of silver, and the money being used to buy a potter's field. He saw God's sword awakened, the Shepherd smitten, the sheep scattered. Yes, and he saw, too, the glorious return of Christ, splitting Olivet asunder and all nations beating a path to His feet. He saw a day when there would be no more Canaanite in the house of the Lord.

Then, one morning Zechariah took his usual walk around the temple. The Jews saw him coming. "Behold this dreamer cometh," they said. "Let us kill him and put an end to his sermons and signs." And so they did, accursed Canaanites that they were.

Well, they got rid of the prophet; but they couldn't get rid of his book. The Spirit of God saw to it that it was added to the Bible itself—its closing phrase anticipating the day when "Holiness unto the Lord" would be engraved on every pot and pan in Jerusalem and all men know that holiness is what it's all about.

MALACHI

Malachi was the John the Baptist of the Old Testament—the voice of one crying in the wilderness. When John, the Lord's disciple, took his pen to write the last book of the New Testament, everyone else was dead. His brother, James, was dead. Old camel knees, James, the Lord's brother, was dead. Peter and Paul had been dead for thirty to thirty-five years. It was the same with Malachi in the Old Testament. When Malachi took his pen to write the last book of the Old Testament, everyone else was dead—Zerubbabel, Joshua, Haggai, Zechariah, Ezra and Nehemiah—all were gone.

To be a prophet of God had always been a lonely business. It must have seemed to Malachi that he was very much alone indeed. The fatal tide of current events had set towards the flood. It was coming in strongly now, and the trend was away from the <u>Torah</u>, away from the Bible, and toward the <u>Talmud</u> and the traditions and teachings of men. By the time of Christ, the Jewish world would be firmly controlled by rabbinical Judaism, by Pharasaical hypocrisy, by legalism and by Sadducean liberalism. It would prove to be a deadly brew against truth incarnate in Christ.

Although Malachi did not date his prophecy, we can arrive at a very possible date. The clue is found in Daniel's famous prophecy of the seventy weeks. From a given date (which turned out to be the date when Artaxerxes signed the decree which permitted Nehemiah to go to Jerusalem and rebuild its walls), three prophetic events were to be dated. <u>One</u> had to do with the murder of the Messiah—He was to be "cut off" after sixty-nine "weeks" (of years) had passed—i.e., after 483 years. <u>One</u> had to do with the Lord's coming return. It focused on one "week" of years—the seven-year period of the coming Antichrist. The <u>other</u> prophesied event was to take place seven "weeks" (i.e., forty-nine years) after the decree of Artaxerxes was signed. The date brings us down to the year 396 B.C. What was so significant about this date? As to <u>that</u>, God remains <u>silent</u>; and <u>that</u> is the whole point of it. After <u>that</u> date, God would remain silent. That was the time when Malachi preached. After that, God remained silent for four hundred years, the period covered by the events long since recorded in Daniel 11.

What did this last prophet have to say? He said that towards their sovereign maker, the people adopted a contradictory attitude, arguing with God. Towards their salvation message, they had adopted a contemptuous attitude—offering their leftovers to God. Towards their separated ministers (the Levites), they had adopted a corrupting attitude. Towards the sanctity of marriage, they had adopted a callous attitude—by the time of Christ, a man could divorce his wife for burning his toast. Towards the sinful majority, they had adopted a complaisant attitude. Towards their secular materialism, they had adopted a carnal attitude, robbing God without compunction or hesitation, and towards their sacred manuscripts, they had adopted a careless attitude. No wonder Malachi preached!

Malachi ends on a disturbing note, even more disturbing for the Jews since the Old Testament came to an end along with his prophecy. Thus both the book of Malachi and the Old Testament end with the sobering word, "Curse!" The Jews did not like it at all so they regrouped the books, putting Malachi elsewhere and ending with Chronicles instead. That did not help them avoid the curse. However, God overruled their action. The long list of names with which 1 Chronicles begins dovetails right into the list of names with which Matthew begins—a list of names which takes us straight to Jesus! So, God began all over again. The Old Testament ends with a curse; the New Testament begins with a cradle. God began to speak again but this time not through mere men alone, this time He spoke through His Son—"the Word made flesh."

JOSEPH AT HOME
GENESIS 30; 35:19; 37:11

Joseph had ten older brothers, one younger brother and a sister. Since Jacob had four wives, all fiercely competitive to give him sons, his children were all close to the same age. Joseph lived in a disorderly home, for his father and mother doted on Joseph; and his older brothers detested him. Let us take a closer look at this home.

First, there was his mother, a very beautiful woman, and one who ruled supreme in Jacob's heart. Doubtless she shielded her beloved Joseph from the malice of his older brothers. She died, however, when Joseph was about seventeen years of age and brokenhearted Joseph was thrown to the wolves. His father was in a fog of loneliness and unhappiness over the death of his dear Rachel and seems unaware of Joseph's peril.

Then there was his aunt Leah, a plain-faced, straight Jane of a woman. Jacob had never loved her with the passion with which he loved Rachel. More, she had married Jacob by being party to a trick promoted by her father, Laban. Many a time, likely enough, Joseph would find Leah crying in some remote corner of the farm. "Never let yourself be used against your better judgment," was the lesson of Leah. "Never do someone a wrong just because that is the easy way out of a difficult situation." That was a lesson he learned well and which stood him in good stead when he was confronted by Potipher's wife.

And what about Grandpa Laban? What a fierce, grasping, unscrupulous, vindictive old man he was. Joseph saw clearly that Laban loved things and used people. Joseph learned from that. He used things and loved people. Moreover, Laban was more than half a pagan. Watching Laban bow down to graven images taught Joseph the folly of idolatry—a valuable lesson when later he was brought into contact with the gross polytheism of Egypt, and was even married to the daughters of a pagan priest.

Just a year before his mother's death, Joseph discovered what a bad lot some of his older brothers were. He was with the four slave-born sons of Bilhah and Zilpah. They were an unscrupulous quartet. Once out of sight of Jacob's encampment, they were up to all kinds of devilry. When Joseph refused to conform to their wicked ways, doubtless, they threatened him: "Don't you dare tell, you smug young psalm singer. We'll kill you." Joseph ignored their threats and told the truth about them. He learned thus how to take a lonely, unpopular stand for God no matter what.

His oldest brother, Reuben, was no help either. He had neither character or courage. Joseph was doubtless aware of Reuben's adulterous affair with Bilhah, one of his father's wives. The sordid business, and Reuben's consequent lifelong fear of being found out, taught Joseph the high price of immorality. He vowed to steer clear of that kind of thing, at all costs. The price tag was too high.

As for Simeon and Levi, Joseph had good cause to fear the pair of them. Simeon was a cruel man, and Levi was even worse for he had a touch of the fanatic about him.

Then there was calculating Judah. "What's in it for me?" was his motto. He was the one who suggested selling Joseph into slavery for twenty silver pieces. No doubt he was motivated by the fear that Jacob would give the double portion of the birthright blessing to Joseph. Judah would have had designs on that for himself.

And what about Dinah, his only sister? Well, she was seduced as a result of some clandestine trips to the nearby town of Schechem and by the friendships she forged with the unsaved. Terrible, indeed, were the consequences. Joseph learned the lesson well—play day is followed by pay day.

But, the dominating member of the family, when all was said and done, was Jacob. Joseph was into his teens, and old enough to learn the value of a new life in Christ, when Jacob came to the Jabbok and was changed from Jacob to Israel. All these things molded and made Joseph, as God knew they would. That is why He put Joseph in that family. He has equally good reasons for putting us in ours.

GO TELL MY FATHER
GENESIS 45:13

The scales had fallen from their eyes, and they knew him at last. "I am Joseph," he said. "You sold. . . . God did send." Then came the challenge. "Go, tell my father of all my glory which ye have seen." That is the very essence of worship, to tell the Father of the beauty of Jesus which we have seen. This challenge was two-fold. First, it required them to EXPOSE THEIR SIN.

The last time they spoke to the father about Joseph was when they brought home Joseph's coat of many colors, all stained with blood. They had thrown it at Jacob's feet and (disowning Joseph) demanded: "Do you know whether or not this is you son's coat?" Now they have to confess. We can well imagine the things they had to say.

"Father, we have seen him, your son. He is alive! We have seen his glory! We hated him, father.

"We hated him for the life that he lived, a life so different from ours. He always did those things that pleased the father and we hated him. He showed us up.

"We hated him for the truth that he taught, especially for those dreams of his which spoke of his exaltation and glory. He declared that every knee would bow to him one day. We hated him.

"We hated him for the witness he was. He brought to you the evil report of our ways. And we were wicked, father. He simply bore faithful witness to what he heard and saw. We hated him.

"We hated him for the authority he assumed. He was your well-beloved son, and he wore that royal robe you gave him like a born prince. He exercised the authority it bestowed, the authority you gave him. We hated him.

"We envied him. We could not speak peaceably to him. He came to us, and we received him not. We sold him for the price of a slate and handed him over to the gentiles." That was how they must have begun—with the exposure of their sin.

But, then, this confession required them to EXALT THE SAVIOR: "Go tell my father of all my glory which ye have seen," Joseph said. They would continue: "Now, father, our eyes have been opened. We see him now, at last, as you have always seen him.

"We have seen the glory of his person. We only saw him before as one of us, engaged in the everyday affairs of life. But now, ah, now! We have seen him enthroned in splendor surrounded and by magnificence beyond anything our imaginations could have conceived. We have been awed by his wisdom, his love and his power. And we have been made the recipients of his grace.

"We have seen the glory of his position. All we have ever known is a Beduin camp; but now, down here in Egypt, we have seen another world, a world the like of which we never dreamed could be, a world of towering pyramids, a world where gold is as common as brass, where power is god-like and where runs a river which brings life to all. We have seen the high throne on which he sits, and we have seen his great and gifted servants rushing to do his will. And now he has a name above every name, and before that name every knee must bow.

"We have seen, too, <u>the glory of his power</u>. He wields absolute power, but he wields it in benevolence and for the blessing of all.

"Finally, father, we have seen <u>the glory of his pardon</u>. He did not, for one moment, excuse our sin; but he covered it with his grace. It was all overruled by God, he said, so that he could become the savior of the world.

"But that is not all. He has arranged that where he is, there we shall be, also."

"Go, tell my father of all my glory which ye have seen," said Joseph to his brothers. "<u>Go tell My father of all my glory which ye have seen</u>," says the Lord Jesus to us.

THE BONES OF JOSEPH
HEBREWS 11:22

Someone has said that, in no less than 150 ways, Joseph is like Jesus. Certainly there are numerous ways this is so. The Holy Spirit, Himself, emphasizes just one of them: "By faith Joseph, when he died, made mention of the departing of the children of Israel and gave commandment concerning his bones." The bones of Joseph are mentioned four times in the Bible.

The first time we meet these bones, we hear them say: GOD WILL BRING YOU OUT (Gen.50:25). There he is on his deathbed with his brothers all gathered around. Though Joseph was one of the great lords of the land, there was to be no state funeral. He spent no money on a costly tomb in Egypt for he had other plans. His brothers crowd around him, eager to know how he intends to leave his wealth. We can imagine their dismay and disappointment when he reads his will and says: "I bequeath you my <u>bones</u>!" Little did they know; but for some four hundred years, those bones would bear silent testimony to a nation of slaves: "God will bring you out of this land." God had promised it to Abraham. Joseph believed it. Israel forgot it. Joseph's bones confirmed it. However it was the promise of <u>coming redemption</u>.

Joseph was offered the treasures and pleasures of Egypt. God, however, had kept him true—as a lonely lad, and as a lord of the land, in the prison and in the palace. <u>Adversity</u> could not conquer him, <u>advancement</u> could not corrupt him. All that Egypt had to offer was his to command—power, position, prosperity, pleasure, praise—all were his. But on his deathbed, we see a man sick to death of Egypt. "God," he said, "will bring you <u>out, out, out</u> of this land." His bones were to remind the Hebrews that they belonged to another country.

"Ye <u>shall</u>," he said, "Ye <u>shall</u> carry up my bones. . ." He wanted to be buried in Canaan. Jacob had insisted on the same thing. One day, the day Christ arose from the dead, there would be a wholesome resurrection of saints in the promised land. Joseph wanted to be there when it happened.

The second time we meet the bones of Joseph, we hear them say: GOD WILL BRING YOU THROUGH (Exod. 13:19). It is the night of the Exodus. The avenging angel has passed through the land. And from the Delta to the mountains of Ethiopia, all Egypt knew that the God of the Hebrews was a God to be feared. The death of every firstborn in the land acted as a spur. They begged the Hebrews to leave and loaded them down with gifts. Everyone was carrying something of value. What do you think Moses was carrying? Some special Egyptian treasure, no doubt. Oh, no! Nothing like that. The Bible says that "Moses took the bones of Joseph with <u>him</u>." He knew their value. All the way from Egypt to Canaan that body, the body of Joseph was a memorial body. It whispered to Moses: "God has brought you <u>out</u>, God will bring you <u>through</u>." In the great crisis experiences along the way, others trembled but Moses trusted, others were conquered by fear but Moses was controlled by faith. He had the bones of Joseph to remind him of God's promises.

The third time we meet the bones of Joseph, we hear them say: GOD WILL BRING YOU IN (Josh. 24:32). In the end Joshua fell heir to Joseph's bones, and he buried them in Canaan. They were at rest at last. God had overcome all obstacles and every foe. The people were at rest.

But Joseph's bones still had something to say. Put your ear to his costly casket. Those bones of his think it a wonderful joke! The Hebrews thought they had got it all when they conquered Canaan, but the bones of Joseph knew better. His foot bone is talking to his ankle bone, his ankle bone is talking to his shin bone: "Now hear the word of the Lord!"

"Sure!" they say. "They've buried us in Canaan, but <u>we're</u> not going to settle down. God will <u>surely</u> visit us and carry <u>up</u> these bones from thence. He brought us <u>in</u> alright, but we are not here to stay. God will surely <u>bring us up</u>. For Joseph died in hope of the resurrection. And so do we.

CALEB

JOSHUA 14:6-15

The Jews divided old age into three stages. From sixty to seventy was "<u>The Commencement</u>" of old age. From seventy to eighty was "hoary-headed" age. At eighty one was said to be "well stricken in years." Caleb was eighty-five when he demanded his inheritance and asked to be given a haunted mountain where the sons of the Anakim ruled. It is never too late to dare something for God. Abraham was seventy-five when he left Ur. Moses was eighty when God met him at the burning bush. John was an old man when he wrote his books.

"I have wholly followed the Lord," was Caleb's word to Joshua. He had followed the Lord FULLY. He had been born in a ghetto in Goshen about the time Moses had fled from Egypt. Oh, how he longed for a Savior! When Moses came back as Israel's kinsman-redeemer, Caleb had become one of his devoted followers. He had been sheltered behind the blood of the Passover lamb. He had been baptized unto Moses in the cloud and in the sea. He had been gathered with God's people around the table in the wilderness. He had feasted on bread from heaven, had drunk water from the riven rock and had smitten Amalek (a type of the flesh) with the edge of the sword. He had even been over Jordan. So, where others saw a diabolical foe, Caleb saw a defeated foe.

His name means "dog"; and like a faithful dog, he wholly followed the Master. He could say, "I have wholly followed the Lord."

Then, too, he followed the Lord FEARLESSLY. Note <u>his calm assessment of the outlook</u>. The way ahead promised to be <u>arduous</u> to take that rocky steep.—it was a mountain he claimed. Caleb knew it would be an uphill fight all the way. It promised to be <u>dangerous</u> for the sons of the

Anakim were there, a hybrid race of giants. It promised to be <u>tedious</u> for the cities were great and fenced, "walled up to heaven," was the way they were described. They would have to be taken by long and stubborn siege. Such was his clear assessment of the outlook. But note, also, <u>his calm assurance of the outlook</u>: "If so be that the Lord will be with me . . ." (He was counting on the Lord's <u>presence</u>), then I shall drive them out, as the Lord hath said. . ." (He was counting on the Lord's <u>promise</u>).

Finally, Caleb had followed the Lord FAITHFULLY. There were no stops and starts in his commitment. Nothing but a steady walk with God.

Years ago, Allan Redpath, a well-known preacher and former pastor of Moody Church, was crossing the Atlantic on the <u>Queen Elizabeth</u>. He made friends with one of the ship's engineers. The man took him down to see the mighty engines roaring and pounding in the depths of the ship. Then he took him back to the stern of the boat where the drive shafts throbbed and screamed as they turned the giant propellers which drove the mighty floating hotel through the water—all 83,000 tons of it.

Back in the chief engineer's cabin, Allan ventured a comment. "I suppose," he said, "those drive shafts and propellers must be going around at an enormous speed!" "It's plain that you are no engineer!" replied the officer. "I could get those propellers going so fast, Allan, that they would just dig a big hole in the water, and the ship would come to a stop. I have forty-eight engineers under me on this ship," he added, "and they are constantly calculating the ratio between revolutions per minute in the engine room and <u>steadiness at the point of drive</u>."

<u>Steadiness</u>! That was the word! That is the word which sums up Caleb. He was steady. He wholly followed the Lord, come what may. May we do the same.

ELI

I SAMUEL 2:27-36

Eli was Israel's high priest in the closing days of the judges, a time when immorality and apostasy went hand in hand. He was Israel's high priest, but he really had no claim to the position at all. He was not descended from the family of Eleazar, to whom the high priesthood belonged, but from the family of Ithamar, Aaron's youngest son. It is typical of the confusion of the time that we have no idea how he came to be high priest. It is typical, also, that his whole career (as recorded in 1 Samuel) was one of utter failure.

First he was a failure as a PERSON. He was old. Young men see visions, the Bible says, and old men dream dreams. Eli dreamed away his days. "His eyes were dim," the Holy Spirit adds. He was blind to the needs of the people. "Where there is no vision, the people perish" the scripture declares. Poor old Eli was blind even to the state of his own family. Typical, too, was his treatment of Hannah. He could not even tell the difference between a drunken woman and a devout worshipper, and he had some harsh words for that broken-hearted soul. His half apology, when he realized his mistake, does him no credit either.

So, there was Eli, old, slothful, worn-out, content to sit in his rocking chair and doze away his days while Israel sank ever deeper in the mire.

Then, too, he was a failure as a PARENT. "His sons," we are told, "made themselves vile." Their behavior was a national scandal. It was not safe for an attractive woman to bring a sacrifice to the altar. She was likely to fall foul of the lawless lusts of Eli's sons. Eli shrugged his shoulders when people complained and went back to sleep.

Then, too, there was their sin against God. The Levitical law set aside a portion of each sacrifice for the officiating priest. The fat, however, was to be burned on the altar. That was God's portion. Eli's unscrupulous sons dared to rob God. They appropriated the fat for themselves. Eli merely slapped their wrists. He should have thrust them out of the priestly office. Instead he indulged them.

Doubtless, he had never curbed them, never taken the rod to them, to break their wills when they were young. They grew up willful and wild, and wicked beyond words. So Eli's failure as a parent was a serious thing for he contributed two unregenerate sons to the priesthood. It brought about the downfall of his house.

Finally and worst of all, he was a failure as a PRIEST. He seems to have had little or nothing to do. He stands in contrast with Samuel, who went up and down the land seeking to arouse an apostate and apathetic people to a sense of sin and need. Eli waited for people to come to him. Few came. So, all we see is a tired, old man dozing in the sun.

The <u>first</u> time we meet him in the Bible he is propped up against a post of the tabernacle idling his life away. The <u>next time</u> we see him he is sound asleep in bed. A little lad, entrusted to his care, had to wake him up three times before it finally dawned on him that God had something to say to the boy. Eli had long since ceased expecting that God might have something to say to him. The <u>last</u> time we see him he is sitting on a chair by the roadside. He fell off that seat and broke his neck. Such was Eli.

But there was one bright spot. He did a good job of bringing up little Samuel. Or did he? Maybe it was not so much due to old Eli that Samuel turned out so well. Perhaps that was a result of his mother's earnest prayers.

WILT THOU GO WITH THIS MAN?
GENESIS 24

The story of Abraham, sending his servant to find a bride for Isaac, is a full-length Old Testament portrait of Christ and His Church.

All the initiative was with Abraham (who stands for the Father). The servant, sent forth into the world to seek the needed bride, represents the Holy Spirit. Isaac, seated with his father, pictures the Lord Jesus.

The servant did not go abroad to speak about himself, only to magnify the father and the son. When he found the prospective bride, he used no coercion. He simply presented the facts and extended an invitation.

He did, however, come bearing gifts. And here the difference between Rebekah and her brother, Laban, is seen. When Laban saw the earrings and the bracelets on his sister's hands, he was all ears and eyes. He wanted such gifts, the spectacular sign gifts which accredited the servant and proved his mission to be valid. He reminds us of Simon Magus who wanted to acquire an apostolic gift for his own enrichment and aggrandizement. It nearly cost him his soul (Acts 8:9-25). Rebekah, by contrast, received the gifts but soon lost interest in them. Her thoughts were not on the gifts, but on the groom.

And so the great question was asked: "Wilt thou go with this man?" "I will," was her simple reply. The story now focuses on the servant and the Bride-to-be. There are four steps in the story.

First, we see <u>Rebekah leaving</u> for there had to be a complete break with the past. All that belonged to her past life became a fading memory. Her thoughts were on the future for she knew that, when her traveling days were done, one would be awaiting her arrival at his home. Where he was, there she would be also. She had never seen him, but she believed in him. The unnamed servant had done his work well. She had the gifts, also, to remind her of the one who was awaiting her.

Next, we see <u>Rebekah learning</u>. The unknown servant (type of the Holy Spirit) was now her comforter and her guide. It was not left up to her to find her way to Isaac and his father's house. It was the responsibility of the servant to bring her safely home. She must have had a thousand questions. He would delight to tell her more and more about the one she had set out to meet. He would tell her of Isaac's miraculous birth and how he was the father's well-beloved and "only begotten" son. He would tell how he had become obedient unto death and how he had came back, as it were, from the dead.

Then we see <u>Rebekah longing</u>. Time passed, and Rebekah's thoughts dwelt less and less on her old life. More and more she focused on the new life she had chosen and on the joy that was set before her. Isaac was both the center and the circumference of her thoughts. The more the servant told her of the father's well-beloved, the more he became increasingly real to her. The more she learned of him, the more she longed for him. And, although she had not seen him, love for him took root in her heart.

Finally, we have <u>Rebekah looking</u>. For, as the journey reached its close, the servant began to prepare her increasingly for the longed-for meeting soon to come. "He will be coming for you," he would say. "It could be any day now. The time of watching and waiting will be over soon." Rebekah would pay more attention to herself, to preparing herself, so that she would be ready when he came, and not be ashamed at his coming. Then one day he came.

And a new chapter in the story of redemption was begun.

THE DEAD SHALL RISE FIRST
1 THESS 4:16

"The dead in Christ shall rise first," God says. That is fair. These are the saints of God who hoped and prayed that the Lord would come while they were still alive, but death came instead. But they have this advantage over those who are alive and remain when Christ comes, they will go up first. "Then we which are alive and remain shall be caught up." Those who are thus raptured will shout, "O death where is thy sting?" Those who come bounding from their graves will sing: "O grave, where is thy victory?" (1 Cor. 15:55). There is no room for doubt. "They shall!" God says. It was all settled in heaven a long time ago. The graves will be plundered of those who are asleep. The globe will be plundered of those who are alive. And the time is drawing nigh.

My wife has a little music box. When it is opened, it plays a little tune—"Raindrops Keep Falling on My Head." The box can be opened. Inside there is a small brass cylinder. That cylinder has a lot of little spikes sticking up all over it. Along with they cylinder and its spikes, there are a number of prongs. Those prongs make the various notes as the rotating spikes on the cylinder hit them.

Now, in a sense, when one looks inside that music box, he can see the whole tune. It is all pegged out, so to speak. But, in order to experience the tune, it is necessary to wait for the process of time to run its course. One has to wait for the slow turning of the cylinder, and for all the little spikes to hit all the corresponding prongs. As the cylinder slowly revolves, the music comes —

PING! PING! PING-A-PING-A-PING!

That is how it is with us and with God. God sees the whole thing—the whole future, so to speak, is all pegged out in heaven. But we are creatures of time. We have to wait for the slow day-by-day process whereby the time-less purposes of God are wrought out in human history and experience.

But God who is omniscient, and who sees everything, and hears everything, and who knows everything sees it all. It is all pegged out in heaven, and it will all be played out on earth. Those spokes will hit the corresponding prongs. The whole tune will be played. The music has already begun. The "Shall!" "Shall!" of God's word is even now coming to pass. A few more notes, and we'll be gone. The dead in Christ <u>shall</u> rise, we who are alive and remain <u>shall</u> be caught up. Nothing can stop it.

That must have been comforting news for the Thessalonian believers. Paul had not been able to stay long in their city. He had been driven out by persecution. He arrived at length in Athens, having sent Timothy back to Thessalonia for news of the infant church. Timothy returned with good news. The church was alive and well. However, some believers had died in the short interval between the expulsion of Paul and the arrival of Timothy. Had they missed the rapture?

"Oh no!" Paul said, "not a bit of it! The contrary was true. All believers would rise to meet the Lord in the air—but the dead in Christ would take precedence. The dead in Christ would rise first." Good news for all!

ELIMELECH: MOVING TO MOAB
RUTH 1:1-5

The events recorded in the book of Ruth seem to have taken place early in the days of the Judges, at a time when the Promised Land was at rest. God's displeasure was evident just the same, being expressed by means of natural phenomena, such as the famine mentioned in the book. They had not yet been sold into bondage to the surrounding foes.

The story revolves around four people: Elimelech, Naomi, Boaz and Ruth. We begin with <u>Elimelech</u> and his family. First, we see them MOVING TO MOAB. It was a disastrous move.

In the Old Testament all God's promises and blessings for His people were centered in a <u>place</u>; in the New Testament they are centered in a <u>Person</u>. In the Old Testament one had to be in <u>Canaan</u>, in the New Testament one has to be in <u>Christ</u>. It was in the Promised Land that God met with His people. It was there He put His name. It was there He made good His promises and centered His purposes. It was a disastrous decision, there-

fore, that Elimelech made to move to Moab. Even more so since Moab was
a land under the curse of God (Deu. 23:3). To move to Moab meant leaving
the fellowship of God's people. It meant removing the family from every
means of grace associated with the company and gathering of God's people, feeble though they seemed to be.

Elimelech's name means "My God is King." That was all well and
good, but he denied the sovereignty of God in his life when he decided to
move to Moab. Doubtless, he had plenty of excuses. "There was a famine
in the Promised Land," he no doubt said. There were job opportunities in
Moab. He did not intend to stay down there. He would be back when
things improved. All the usual things people say, to encourage themselves
in pursuing a wrong path, were likely said by Elimelech.

Next, we have MARRIAGE IN MOAB. Instead of growing to man-
hood surrounded by young Hebrew women, Elimelech's boys had pagan
girls only from whom to choose a partner for life. Their in-laws were raw
heathen and their chief god was the diabolical and bloodthirsty Moloch,
the devourer of little children. It was just as well that both Elimelech's sons
were sickly and that they had no children of their own. Moses would have
been all against marrying in Moab (Deut 7:3) or any other kind of marriage
with unbelievers.

But then comes MISERY IN MOAB. Elimelech died. Then his two
sickly boys died; and Naomi, now a bitter, old woman, "was left." That's
how the Holy Spirit puts it—left, stranded in a foreign country with a couple of unsaved, widowed daughters-in-law. The breadwinners were gone.
Naomi was out of the will of God, far from the place where God met with
His people and she was surrounded by pagans in a heathen land. Such was
the end of Elimelech's backsliding. He lost his life in Moab, and he lost his
family in Moab. The cost of backsliding is high. His good intentions of
returning to the Promised Land never materialized.

Moab is an expensive place to raise a family. Those who leave the
house of God, and who wander off into the world, will stand the risk of los-
ing their children. And they died there, far from the fellowship of the people
of God. How solemn, and how sad! The New Testament makes it a doc-
trine: "Be ye not unequally yoked together with unbelievers: for what fellowship hath righteousness with unrighteousness? and what communion
hath light with darkness? and what concord hath Christ with Belial? or what

part hath he that believeth with an infidel? and what agreement hath the temple of God with idols? for ye are the temple of the living God" (2 Cor. 6:14-16).

NAOMI FINDS GRACE
RUTH 1:6-17

The world, as represented by Moab, opened its arms to Elimelech the backslider. He settled down in that dark and dangerous place. He lost his sons to Moab. As Moab had once, years before, seduced the men of Israel with the women of Moab, so now Moab seduced the sons of Elimelech with the same bait. Elimelech's sons were quite content to live in Moab, to marry in Moab and, in the end, to die in Moab and be buried in Moab. And so they did, far from God, their consciences silenced, their convictions, if they ever had any, seduced, and their days shortened.

Naomi lived through it all, growing more and more desolate, lonely and embittered as time went on. Her only solace was that her two daughters-in-law respected her and treated her well. Ten years wore wearily away. Graves were dug. Husbands and sons were buried. And all about her the Moabites went about their business and carried on their dark religion. The priests of Ashteroth enslaved little girls into prostitution for the worship of Baal and the priests of Moloch seized little boys to be offered living on the red-hot lap of their fierce and fiery god. Ten weary years. And then a change came.

We think, first, of Naomi's TIDINGS. She heard from home. The famine was over! The fields bore promise of a bumper harvest! God had been visiting His people! Revival had come! Naomi made up her mind. She would go home. Backsliding had beggared and embittered her but her heart was still hungry for the place where God had put His name. She would go home and take her place once more with the people of God.

We think, also of Naomi's TESTIMONY. She told her two daughters-in-law of her decision. She was sick to death of Moab. She intended to get right with God, with the true and living God of her people. She would say "good-bye" to them. All backsliding had done for her was rob her and ruin her.

"Mara" (Bitter) should be her true name, not Naomi (Pleasant). Gone was the blessing associated with the name Naomi. Instead had come the bitterness associated with the name "Mara." Such was her unpromising testimony.

Poor as it was, however, it bore fruit. Both Ruth and Orpah were impressed by the sudden change in Naomi. They both declared that they would come as well. However like the backslider she still was, Naomi tried to discourage them. "You would do better stay in Moab," she said. "You'll never get remarried if you come with me. I can't think of a self-respecting Jew who would marry a Moabite." It was terrible advice. It should warn us never to take advice from a backslider. A backslider is a dangerous person no matter who he is or where he is. Abraham's backsliding imperiled Sara (Gen. 12:11-20). Lot's backsliding destroyed his family (Gen.13:8-13; 19:1-38). Jonah's backsliding put others in peril (Jonah 1:4-16).

In Orpah's case Naomi's words were all too successful. She took Naomi's advice and went back to the nightmare darkness of Moab, back to the demon gods of her people; and we read of her no more. Ever afterwards, we can be sure, Naomi had Orpah's lost soul on her conscience. It would haunt her and grieve her beyond words.

But Ruth was made of sterner stuff. She had seen glimpses of God in Naomi. And she liked what she had seen. "I'm coming," she said. "I want to know more of your God and His people." And so she did. Thus God brought something good out of it after all—a precious soul, a woman who would find her place among God's redeemed people and who would help move forward the coming of the Christ of God.

ORPAH FALLS FROM GRACE
RUTH 1:11-15

Orpah turned back, and it was impossible to renew her again unto repentance. God blots her name out of His book, and we read of her no more. Her story revolves around three choices.

There was, for instance, HER FIRST CHOICE. It was to marry into a family of believers. She came to know the family very well. Often around the family supper table she would hear Elimelech and Naomi talk nostalgically about the true and living God, how He had sent them a kinsman-redeemer to deliver them from bondage and death. He had put them under the blood, He had brought them through the water and He had gathered them around the table. He had given them His laws and had given them their land. She listened to their Bible stories, fascinating and factual stories, about Adam and Even, Enoch and Noah, Abraham, Isaac and Jacob. She heard about God's wisdom, love and power. But, alas for Orpah, she was wedded to her idols. Truth penetrated her mind but never touched her heart.

So Orpah made her first choice. She married into the only family in Moab which had personal knowledge of God. Before her lay the opportunity of coming to know that God for herself.

The came HER FURTHER CHOICE. Sorrow came into her life. Death came calling again and again until Naomi, Ruth and Orpah all became widows. Then Naomi decided she'd had enough. News that God had been visiting His people, back there in Bethlehem, helped her make her decision. She would return to her people and her God, and then it was that Orpah made her second choice. She would go with Naomi. Naomi's God would become her God, and Naomi's people would become her people. Ruth made the same decision. So far, so good. But everything would hinge on what happened next. The three widows said their last, sad farewells at the graves of their departed loved ones and set their faces towards the Promised Land.

But now comes the tragedy in Orpah's life—HER FINAL CHOICE. She began to lag behind. Naomi's warning about there being little or no hope of remarriage among the Hebrews took over her mind. Perhaps it would be best to go back to Moab. At least she might find a Moabite husband; and, after all, she was a Moabite. She came to a stop, and the other two came back; but Orpah had made up her mind. She would go back to her people and her gods. And so she did. The call of the true God faded away in her soul. She went back to seek rest with a Moabite husband.

Let us suppose that, still young and attractive, she married a Moabite man. Let us suppose, too, she did find rest in his house. What kind of rest would it be? Just temporal rest, at best. A good measure of peace and quiet, a share of this world's goods, perhaps, enjoyment of this world's pleasures and pastimes, attendance at the more pacific and harmless rituals at the local temples and shrines. And a Christless death.

But there was a darker side to pagan religion, one which Orpah seems to have forgotten. Perhaps Orpah gave birth to a girl, a pretty girl with the earthly promise of beauty of face and form. The priests of Astarte and Baal would mark her for the temple, to become a harlot, consecrated to the foul Moabite gods and to be debauched by priests and people alike. And Orpah's rest was gone forever.

Or, perhaps, Orpah gave birth to a boy. Terror would seize her soul as the boy began to grow. The priest of Moloch might cast his evil eye on her little boy and put a mark on him: "Bring him to me at the temple tomorrow," he might say. "We'll find a place for him on Moloch's lap. You are a woman favored of the god." What then about Orpah's rest? Gone! Forever gone. It was a terrible choice she made—to settle for the world's uneasy peace.

BOAZ FINDS A WAY

Love always finds a way. As the hymn-writer puts it:[1]

> *"Love found a way to redeem my soul.*
> *Love found a way that could make me whole.*
> *Love took my Lord to the cross of shame.*
> *Love found a way—oh bless His holy Name."*

"Love never faileth." That, says the Holy Spirit, is the nature of love.

There can be no doubt that Boaz loved Ruth, right from the start, even before he actually met her there in the harvest field. "All the city of my people doth know that thou art a virtuous woman," he said. He knew all about her. His heart was already stirred.

And then he met her. "The servant that was set over the reapers," told Boaz who she was. In the Old Testament an unnamed servant is often a type of the Holy Spirit. It was this unnamed servant who made the introduction, that momentous face to face meeting at which Boaz's heart went out to Ruth. He gave her ample evidence of the state of his heart. He gave her an ephah of grain, ten times what she needed. He would marry her! In spite of the obstacles! And there were four of them. And formidable obstacles they were. But love found a way.

The first obstacle was the fact of A CURSED RACE. For Ruth was a Moabite, and the Moabites were a people under the curse of God. The reason was historical (Deut.3-6). When the Hebrews reached the Moabite frontier, on their way from Egypt to Canaan, the Moabites opposed them. In fact, they hired a Mesopotamian psychic to come and curse them. When that failed, they corrupted them and then looked for God to curse them for their sin. God punished the fallen Israelites, indeed; but He brought a curse down upon the Moabite race. But that was only part of it. The curse of the Law upon the Moabite people was but the <u>fruit</u>. The <u>root</u> of the curse went much deeper and ran back some 550 years or so. For the father of Moab was Lot. Moab was the son incestuously conceived of Lot's oldest daughter on the hills overlooking the smoldering ruins of Sodom, and his godless descendants (the Moabites) became Israel's determined foes.

But there was another obstacle for Boaz. It was the obstacle of a CONDEMNING RULE. For the Law legislated against the Moabite: "An Ammonite or a Moabite shall not enter into the congregation of the Lord, even to their tenth generation shall they not enter, for ever. . . Thou shalt not seek their peace nor their prosperity all thy days forever" (Deut.23:3-6). That was indeed a formidable obstacle. Only the bringing into operation a higher law (the law of the kinsman-redeemer) could find a way around it.

Then, too, there was the obstacle of a CLOSER RELATIVE. Boaz had to be very careful in working his way around this obstacle. Two issues were involved. First there was the matter of the <u>property</u>, (the property of Elimelech which was in limbo now that his sons, Mahlon and Chilion were now also dead). The nearer kinsman was eager to make sure of that.

Then, suddenly, Boaz raised the other issue, the matter of the <u>person</u>. The nearer kinsman could not have the property without the person. If he wanted to acquire the property he would have to wed the widow Ruth. He backed off in a hurry. He certainly did not want to wed a cursed Moabite. The last thing he wanted was to mar his family tree, and spoil his hope of becoming an ancestor of Christ, by introducing Moabite blood into his ancestral line. Boaz had no such scruples. His family tree was already "marred." His mother was the Canaanite harlot, Rahab.

Finally, there was the obstacle of a COSTLY REQUIREMENT. As kinsman redeemer he would be obliged to buy both the person and the property of Ruth. Redemption was a costly business. Boaz, however, was both able and willing to pay the price for he was a "mighty man of wealth" and he loved the Moabite widow with all his heart. So love found a way. The obstacles were swept aside, Boaz married the Moabite and the stage was set for the coming of Christ.

¹Ava B. Christiansen, "Wonderful Love That Rescued Me" (Great Hymns of the Christian Faith, John Peterson, Ed. Singspiration, Inc., Zondervan, Grand Rapid, 1968), Hymn No. 471.

RUTH FINDS BOAZ
RUTH 2:10

When we first meet Ruth, she is in the far country, an alien from God and a stranger to grace. Unlike the prodigal son, she did not <u>burst</u> into the far country. He came there pursuing pleasure and wasting his substance with riotous living. Ruth was <u>born</u> in the far country so she knew, from her own experience, what an empty place it was. To Ruth, the "far country" was Canaan, a longed-for land of life and rest where people worshipped the true and living God, not the fierce and filthy gods of Moab.

Perhaps she had dreamed of such a place in her younger days. If so, the place of her dreams was a faraway country, indeed, known to no one in Moab. If so, too, her meeting with one of Elimelech's sons must have given sudden form and substance to her dreams. For he had been born in that country. He and his parents could give it shape and form as well as a name—Canaan, the Promised Land.

So she married into this family and listened eagerly to the tales Naomi told and to the truths Elimelech taught until the death of her husband faced her with the challenge of a change. When Naomi announced her decision to go back home to her people and her God, Ruth made up her mind. She would go with her to the land of her dreams.

Then Boaz, the kinsman-redeemer, the mighty man of wealth, came into her life. Desperately poor, she took advantage of the land laws of Israel and went into the fields to glean. It so happened, we are told, that she chose a field that belonged to Boaz, a man she did not know but who was soon to fill her life.

We find her, then, in the FIELD OF BOAZ. She had come a long way. Up to now she had never heard his name. She knew little of the Hebrew law of the kinsman-redeemer. Possibly Elimelech and Naomi had told her about Moses who had become a kinsman-redeemer to Israel. (Moses exemplifies redemption by power; Boaz depicts redemption by purchase). Perhaps she had heard of these things from Naomi. Even so she would still not know how they could relate to her. But, at least, she was now in his field. And while Ruth knew little or nothing about these things, Boaz most certainly did.

She must have been astonished to discover that Boaz knew all about her. More than that, he poured out his grace upon her, made provision for her and sent her home laden down with good things.

Next, we find her at THE FEET OF BOAZ. "The man is near of kin unto us," Naomi said when Ruth arrived home bursting with news. For she saw it at once! The law of the kinsman-redeemer opened every door. Naomi, back in fellowship with God's people, was now able to give good and godly advise to Ruth. "You must go to this man," she said, "you must put yourself at his feet and ask to be redeemed. You must invoke the law and ask Boaz to marry you." Not that Boaz would need to be reminded of the law! He was already in love with Ruth. Love, not law, would guide his steps now. So Ruth came to Boaz, just as she was, in all her need and put herself at his feet.

Finally, we see her in THE FAMILY OF BOAZ. The claims of the law had to be met, especially the rules and regulations connected with the role and responsibilities of a kinsman-redeemer. There was no way Ruth could fulfill the law's demands. The law legislated against her in a most forceful way since she was a Moabite. But Boaz could meet the law's demands, and he did. Then he paid the price of Ruth's redemption and purchased both her person and her late husband's property. Then Boaz married her and put her in his family and gave her a living link to Christ. All of which, of course, and much more beside, Jesus does for us.

RUTH FINDS REST

Orpah sought rest in Moab, but she sought it there in vain. For rest is centered in a person, not a place; and Orpah never found that person. Ruth did. She met Boaz, and her life was never the same again. It was Naomi, the restored backslider, who taught Ruth how to find her rest in Boaz.

First, there had to be CLEANSING. "Wash thyself," she said. Obviously Ruth could not go to Boaz bathed in perspiration from a hard day's gleaning in the field. Gleaning was hot, hard work. It involved a great deal of physical activity—bending and stretching, cutting and gathering—all through the burden and heat of the day. She needed to be cleansed from all that.

"Wash thyself!" When God sought to convey to the Hebrew people the fact of sin's defilement, He did so by means of the tabernacle. At one end He sat in the holy of holies, enthroned in unimpeachable righteousness and holiness. At the other end stood the guilty sinner. Between them stood the brazen altar and the brazen laver, <u>blood</u> and <u>water</u>.

A sinner could approach God only by way of the altar and the laver. He would arrive first at the brazen altar to present his sin offering or His trespass offering. Blood was shed. He recognized the fact that there had to be a <u>radical</u> cleansing from sin. Next (if he was a priest) he came to the brazen laver which was made of the mirrors of the women. He saw at once that he had been defiled in his walk, even going that short way. He needed a <u>renewed</u> cleansing from sin. He needed what Paul would later call, "the washing of water by the word." "Wash yourself," said Naomi to Ruth. And so she did.

Next, came CONSECRATION. "Anoint thee!" Naomi said. Anointing, in both the Old and New Testaments, points us to the Person and work of the Holy Spirit. There must be no odor of the flesh about us when we come to our heavenly Boaz seeking rest. There must be a fragrance of God about us. Mary of Bethany could tell us about that. She brought her alabaster flask of costly perfume and used that precious ointment to anoint the Lord Jesus. Instantly the whole house was filled with fragrance. Likewise Ruth was taught to come to Boaz bearing the fragrance of one anointed. It advertised her presence in a bold but silent, unmistakable and pleasing way.

Finally, there was CHARACTER: "Put thy raiment upon thee," said Naomi. This raiment was evidently not the one she wore to work, stained with sweat, drenched with perspiration. No, indeed! This raiment was fresh and fit for the master's house. In the symbolism of the Bible, raiment speaks of character. We are to "put off" the old man and his deeds and "put on" the new man. Ruth's true character was already known to Boaz. He had already acknowledged her to be a virtuous woman.

Thus prepared, Ruth came to Boaz; and he responded at once. Before long, he took her to himself and made her his very own. All of which points us to Christ. When we are united to Him we can sing in the words of the gospel hymn:

"I came to Jesus as I was
Weary and worn and sad
I found in Him a resting place
And He has made me glad."

AHITHOPHEL, DAVID'S JUDAS
II SAMUEL 15:12, 31; 17:23

God forgave David, both for the seduction of Bathsheba and for the slaughter of Uriah. God forgave him, but Ahithopel never did. Ahithophel died a suicide, cursing David, but with crimes on his conscience far exceeding anything David had on his. He died on a gallows in Giloh. He died nursing a malice and hatred for David which beggars description. And thereon hangs a tale.

We are prone to think of David as a type of Christ, and rightly so, for he was a type of Christ in many ways, especially in his early years when he was "a man after God's own heart." But there was another side to David, as there is with all of us. And it is this other side which is brought so sharply into focus in his contacts with Ahithophel. There are three aspects to the story.

We begin with DAVID'S FRIEND. In one of his great psalms, David describes Ahithophel as "my own familiar friend in whom I trusted, which did eat of my bread" (Ps.41:9). In another psalm he calls him "a man mine equal, my guide, my acquaintance, we took sweet counsel together and walked unto the house of God in company" (Ps.55:12-14). It was no accident that David chose this man to be his primary counsellor, for Ahithopel had a great deal to contribute to David. He was the cleverest man in the country; and, at times, his advice was little short of inspired. Moreover, he was not only David's counsellor, he was David's companion, they would walk together to the house of God. He was also David's confidant. David would share his secret dreams and desires with him, his plans for the future of the kingdom.

But then, Ahithophel became DAVID'S FOE, his bitterest, most malignant and formidable foe. Absalom's rebellion would never have got off the ground had not Ahithophel gone over to his side. Ahithopel had two main objectives in mind when he went over to Absalom. He wanted David's wives, those left behind in Jerusalem, to be publicly seduced by Absalom, on the roof top of the palace, before the public gaze. His goal was to make sure that the alienation between David and Absalom was beyond any reconciliation. His second, if not his primary goal, was to kill David. When David was in full flight from Jerusalem, Ahithophel pleaded with Absalom to let him take a band of soldiers on a swift expedition to corner and kill David before David could organize his own forces. Such was the fierce hatred which now burned in the heart of Ahithophel towards the man to whom he had once professed love and loyalty.

But why the change? The answer lies in DAVID'S FOLLY. It was folly in David to loll around the palace when his soldiers were off to war. It was folly in David, when he caught a glimpse of Bathsheba in her bathrobe, to venture a second look. It was folly for him to seek an introduction to the woman, and to cultivate the acquaintance, especially when he discovered she was married, and married, no less to Uriah, one of his personal body-guards. It was folly supreme to seduce her and criminal folly to kill her husband in order to marry her. For <u>Bathsheba's grandfather was Ahithophel</u>.

One does not need to be a prophet, or the son of a prophet, to imagine how Ahithophel took the seduction of his granddaughter and the murder of her husband. He did his best to pay David back with seduction and succeeded, and he did his best to murder David and very likely would have succeeded if Absalom had been anything like a general.

We know what David said when news of Ahithophel's treason was brought. He prayed God to turn Ahithophel's counsel to foolishness. But, we wonder, what did he say to Bathsheba, when news of Ahithophel's suicide was brought to him. His old friend, his valued counsellor, Bathsheba's old grandfather. What did he say? What will we say when our sins thus terribly find us out?

LOVE THAT KNOWS NO MEASURE
EPHESIANS 3:17-19

Paul's prayer for us is that we might know the breadth, length, depth and height of God's love. Many a person in Paul's place might have questioned God's love. For Paul was in prison, in Rome, accused of high treason, awaiting trial before Nero, longing to be set free. Either to be set free by <u>acquittal</u>, free to get back into the thick of things, on the cutting edge of danger, blazing new gospel trails in "the regions beyond" where lived untold millions still untold. Or set free by <u>death</u> to be welcomed home to his mansion on high. In the meantime, he would bathe in God's limitless love. He prayed that all God's people might do the same.

He prayed that we might know the BREADTH OF GOD'S LOVE. For there is nothing narrow about God's love for people. Jesus loved the publicans and sinners. He loved the wayward prodigal, and He loved his bitter older brother. He loved Judas as much as He loved John. He loved Pilate as much as Peter, Annas and Antipas as much as Andrew and Ananias. Such is God's love. It is wonderfully wide. God loves the world John tells us (Jn. 3:16).

Paul prayed that we might know the LENGTH OF GOD'S LOVE. For how long does God love us? When, for instance, did God <u>start</u> loving us? Was it when we were saved? when we first responded to the Holy Spirit's call? Was it when we were born? Was it when He saw us "in Adam?" Was it when He made the worlds? Was it when He decided, before the foundation of the world, to act in creation and, subsequently, to act in redemption? No, He loved us long before that. His is an everlasting love, a love without a beginning, as eternal as He Himself is.

When will God <u>stop</u> loving us? When we disobey Him, perhaps, or when we fall into sin? Or if we keep on sinning? In that case, will He allow us to plead for forgiveness for only seven times seventy of times? Has He stopped loving the lost in the black eternal darkness of endless night? No! But for them it is His holiness which must rule in equal force as His love.

Paul prayed, too, that we might know the DEPTH OF GOD'S LOVE. How deep is that love? Well, Jesus stepped off the throne of the universe and came <u>down</u>. He came from glory to Galilee, from Galilee to Gethsemane, from Gethsemane to Gabbatha, from Gabbatha to Golgotha, from Golgotha to the grave. <u>That</u> was a long way down.

In the old days, when a sailing ship crept around the world, it had to keep close to the shore. A linesman would stand in the bow of the boat and cast a weighted line into the sea. He would report his findings on how deep or how shallow the water was beneath the keel. The best word was: "No bottom with this line." Such is the love of Christ: "No bottom!" All our sounding lines are far too short to measure the depths to which He was willing to go, and the unfathomable depths of His love—for us.

Finally, Paul prayed that God's people might know the HEIGHT OF GOD'S LOVE. He has now ascended on high, seated in the highest heaven. His throne is high and lifted up. He reigns midst scenes of splendor. Angel hosts bow down to Him. Bright, sinless beings rush to do His will. He basks in His Father's love. Has He now forgotten us? Oh, no! He has seated us with Himself in the heavenlies. Such is His love.

"How good is the God we adore?
Our faithful, unchangeable Friend,
Whose love is as great as His power,
And knows neither measure nor end."

SAMUEL THE PROPHET
1 SAMUEL 1:25; 3:20; 7:15-17

Samuel's name is listed among the giants of the faith in Hebrews 11. He was the last of the judges and the first of the prophets. Compared with others of his day, he was a veritable spiritual giant. He was a far greater threat to the Philistines, the hereditary foes of Israel, than ever Samson was, for all of Samson's exploits and practical jokes. Samuel towered head and shoulders above King Saul and helped launch the illustrious David on his triumphant way.

We begin with his MOTHER. Hannah was a remarkable woman, a woman full of faith, able to lay hold of God until assured her barrenness would be turned into blessedness. Included in her pleas for a son was a promise to God to give that son back to God. When the little boy was born, she called him Samuel, which means "asked of God." The name was to remind her, when the temptation came to keep him, that he was not <u>hers</u>, he was <u>His</u>. He was God's.

Then there was his MENTOR, the old priest, Eli, a man who became a second father to Samuel. Eli had done very badly in raising his own sons, but he did exceedingly well in raising Samuel. Soon all Israel knew that a new prophet had arisen, one who knew God and who, young as he was, could speak for God. It was Eli who taught and trained the boy; but it was his mother who prayed for him, for her growing, "Asked of God," now wholly given to God.

We think, too, of his MINISTRY. He lived in a very dark day. There was no king in Israel; and there was no prophet, except himself, to speak for God. The priesthood was in a shambles, and the period of the judges was coming to its inglorious end. The people had been on a seesaw for centuries, up and down, up and down, getting nowhere and ringed in by fierce and implacable foes. The knowledge of the true and living God lingered in the land, but a revival was needed. And Samuel was the man to bring it.

We find that when <u>the will of God was to be sought</u>, it was Samuel who travailed in prayer to ascertain when and where and how this or that or the other thing should be done. It was Samuel who wrestled with God over the matter of the constitutional change of Israel from a theocracy into a monarchy. It was Samuel who wrestled with God over the matter of terminating Saul's infant dynasty and transferring the kingdom to David.

Moreover, when <u>the wars of God were to be fought</u>, it was Samuel who stood in the gap. It was Samuel who fought the Philistines and proclaimed his "Ebenezer" saying, "Hitherto hath the Lord helped us." Never again, in the days of Samuel, after his last, spectacular victory, did the Philistines dare invade Israel. He was a greater man than Samson after all.

Then, too, when <u>the Word of God was to be taught</u>, it was Samuel who taught it. He became Israel's first prophet. Soon all Israel, from Dan to Beersheba, knew that Samuel was established to be a prophet of the Lord. He established a teaching itinerary. He traveled to Bethel, to Gilgal, to Mizpeh and back to Ramah in circuit judging Israel and trying to bring Israel back to the book.

Until, at last, full of years, the aged prophet died; and all Israel wept. And well they might for such men are rare. They occur in every generation; but generally they stand alone, giants in the earth. "Time would fail to tell of Samuel," is the Holy Spirit's last word about Samuel (Heb. 11:32). And so it would. We shall have to wait, therefore, till time shall be no more to hear the rest of this story.

LONELINESS

Samuel Taylor Collerage is famous for having written a picturesque poem about an ancient mariner who set sail for a distant shore. An albatross followed the ship, mile after endless mile. The mariner shot it. At once the helpful wind died away, and the ship became becalmed. The sailors put two and two together. The albatross had brought the wind. Their messmate had killed the albatross. The wind had died with the bird.

In time the sailors began to die of thirst and they died cursing the ancient mariner. At last he alone was left. There was nothing to do, nowhere to go, no one to talk to. He was alone with his remorse. As he told the wedding guest he had waylaid, he was:

> *"Alone, alone, all, all alone*
> *Alone on a wild, wild sea,*
> *And ne'er a soul to take pity on*
> *My soul in agony."*

Loneliness is indeed a visitor to be feared. And often, once it comes, it stays. There is the loneliness of a young man, far from home and friends, wandering the shops and malls of a foreign city, surrounded by people but never a one to be his friend. There is loneliness of a childless widow wandering the rooms of a home that has now become a house filled with dead furniture, haunting memories and crucified hopes.

The psalmist had tasted loneliness. He describes himself as being a lost "pelican in the wilderness." A pelican belongs on a seashore, not in the wild wastes of the wilderness. He was like a lost owl, "like an owl in the desert", he says. An owl belongs where there are forests and fields. He was like a lost sparrow, "a sparrow alone on the housetop." A sparrow belongs in the noisy, busy fellowship of its kind (Ps.102).

Jesus knew what it was like to be lonely. It came over Him overwhelmingly at times. In a graphic statement, unfortunately spoiled by a chapter division, we read: "Every man went to his own home. . ." Jesus went to the Mount of Olives (Jn. 8:53; 9:1). Foxes had their holes; and the birds of the air had their nests, but Jesus had nowhere to lay His head.

And who among us has ever fathomed the depths of His dreadful cry on the cross: "My God, My God, why hast Thou forsaken Me?" (Matt.27:46) That was at the end of his ministry. It had its echo in the dark days of His temptation at the beginning of His ministry.

Mark tells us that Jesus "was there in the wilderness, tempted of Satan, and was with the wild beasts" (Mk.13:13). Perhaps Satan sent them, as the Romans sent starving beasts into the arena to devour the Christians. If Satan imagined Jesus would be attacked by wild beasts, he was very much mistaken. They would be tame as lambs to Him and companions for a while in His loneliness. Then, they, too, went away; and the angels came.

By that time, the Lord was at the end of His strength, starving from a forty-day fast, exhausted from a titanic battle with the evil one. The beasts! The angels! Where was Peter? Where was John? Where were the Twelve? He was alone.

So now, as our Great High Priest in heaven, He has a personal knowledge of what it is like to be lonely! And He does something about it. On the level of His humanity, He shows us ways out of our loneliness. "He who would have friends must show himself friendly," He says (Prov.18:24). There are millions of lonely and needy people. We can seek out some of them to befriend. And on the level of His deity He adds: "And there is a Friend that sticketh closer than a brother." Yes, indeed! What a Friend we have in Jesus, all our griefs and pains to bear! He will never leave us or forsake us. He is our faithful, unchangeable Friend.

SAMSON, THE HEBREW HERCULES
HEBREWS 11:32

He was the Hebrew Hercules, a might man of strength, who rejoiced in his strength and who loved to use it to make mock of the foes of the people of God. His name was Samson. His name means "shining like the sun." And that gives us a clue as to how we should view his spectacular life.

We begin with THE MORNING SUNRISE of his life, a morning full of promise, such promise indeed as might have made him the greatest type of Christ in the entire Old Testament. And even yet, though sadly tarnished by his shortcomings and sins, flashes of his Christlikeness shine through.

At first, all was of Christ. His birth was foretold, like that of Jesus; and, like His, it was a miracle birth. He grew up in seclusion under the blessing of God, and the Spirit of God rested upon him. Indeed the Spirit of God is mentioned more in connection with Samson than with all the other judges combined.

And, like Christ, He was set apart from before his birth to be wholly dedicated to God. He was to be a lifelong Nazarite. His long hair proclaimed that in his very appearance he could easily be recognized as God's man. His abstinence from wine meant his appetites were under control. He did not act from the stimulus of nature but from the empowering of the Holy Spirit. His separation from dead bodies, even those of his nearest and dearest, meant that his affections were on the altar. God came first.

Still as a type of Christ, he took a gentile bride and loved her, weak and apt to betray him as she was. To get that bride, he came to grips with a lion and tore it to pieces and then brought sweetness out of death itself. This became a riddle (a mystery parable indeed) to the Philistines who, at last, had to go to Samson's bride to learn what Samson meant.

Next comes THE MERIDIAN SPLENDOR of his life. The joy of the Lord was his strength. The inner source of his extraordinary power was the Spirit of God. The outward sign of his consecration was his long hair.

As the Lord was rejected by the religious establishment, so it was with Samson. The elders of Israel did not value him. They saw him as a threat. They were afraid his activities would stir up their conquering gentile overlords. So they conspired to hand him over to the Philistines. The enemy, however, was no match for him. He tore away the bonds with which he had been bound, seized the jawbone of an ass, and triumphed gloriously. Then, miraculously, water flowed from that vehicle of death, that old dead jawbone. Similarly, the cross became the despised instrument whereby the foe was conquered and the living water of the Spirit was set free to flow.

But then we see THE EVENING SHADOWS of his life. Women became more and more prominent in Samson's life, pagan, godless women. There was, for instance, the harlot at Gaza. How that liaison must have grieved the Spirit of God. Just the same, He did not depart from him at once but gave him a great victory. His carrying away of the gates of Gaza is a shadowy picture of Christ prevailing over the very gates of hell.

But then Delilah came, and the handwriting was on the wall for Samson. He had played the fool with women once too often. Besides, the Philistines now had the measure of their man. They realized that their men were no match for Samson. They decided to use a woman, to overthrow him, one who was in their pay. Samson became besotted with her. All she wanted was the secret of his power; and, at last, she wheedled it from him. That was the end. The enemy overthrew him, blinded him, and bound him, then set him to work to grind corn, women's work in the East. Then they planned a grandstand occasion to show him off in his shame.

But now comes THE GORY SUNSET of his life. Round and round the millstone went the fallen hero, the object of derision and scorn. "Howbeit," says the Holy Spirit, "the hair of his head began to grow again." The festive day arrived, a public holiday to gloat and triumph over the fallen giant. The Philistine temple was packed. "One more time! Samson pleaded, "Oh, dear God, just one more time!" God granted his prayer. The Spirit came upon Samson and with one more, last, mighty effort down came the temple, posts, pillars, people and all. It was a gory sunset indeed.

But a red sunset heralds the coming of a new and better day. Mighty was Samson's triumph in death. Mighty, too, the victory in death of Jesus, Sun of righteousness, Who in His death and resurrection took captivity captive and gave gifts unto men. Samson's gift to Israel was the dawn of a new day. For Samuel came, and the dark days of the judges were done. The Lord's gift to mankind was a new age of grace—soon to end, now, with an even brighter millennial age to come.

"SEEST THOU THIS WOMAN?"

LUKE 7:44-47

"Seest thou this woman?" One senses a note of sarcasm in the question. "Seest thou this woman?" The man had seen nothing else for the past half hour.

One wonders why this Pharisee invited Jesus to his home in the first place. He offered Him none of the normal courtesies incumbent on a host. His behavior was a deliberate insult to his invited Guest. A thousand angels would have rushed to wash those feet, to give Him a welcoming embrace, to anoint Him with fragrant oil. The Pharisee, instead, had offered the Lord a gratuitous insult. And the Lord recognized it for what it was, and bided His time, for He loved this mean-minded man as much as He loved Peter, James and John. When He spoke, it would be as opportunity gave occasion and with a deep desire to save this small man's soul.

"Seest thou this woman?" She had set before the haughty, self-righteous Pharisee a threefold lesson; and the Lord picked it up at once and applied it to the Pharisee in a threefold repetition of the little word "but."

1. A Lesson in Contrition

"Thou gavest me no water for my feet <u>but</u> she hath washed my feet with her tears, and wiped them with the hairs of her head." "A broken and a contrite heart," said the penitent psalmist, "thou wilt not despise." "She is a sinner!" That was all the Pharisee saw, a woman of the streets who had come into his house uninvited and whom he despised and would gladly have whipped and thrown back on the street. The Pharisee curled his lips in a sneer. "This man is no prophet," he confided to himself, "or He would have known her for a sinner."

Well, God be praised, that is exactly what He did know. He accepted her tears of contrition as fitting tribute to Himself, the One who "came into the world to save sinners."

2.   A Lesson in Consecration

"Thou gavest me no kiss <u>but</u> this woman since the time I came in hath not ceased to kiss my feet," Jesus said. She dared not give Him the customary kiss upon the cheek so down she went at His feet, taking the place of a conquered captive. All her misdirected love was now channeled aright. She was His slave. She kissed His feet in total surrender, while the Pharisee shuddered in his shriveled soul, thinking not of consecration but of contamination. What would all his friends say? A woman like that, in his house.

3.   A Lesson in Coronation

"My head with oil thou didst not anoint, <u>but</u> this woman hath anointed my feet . . ." She recognized Him as the Christ, the Lord's anointed. She poured her ointment over His feet. She crowned Him Lord of all, and Jesus sent her away in peace. Peace means the war is over. From now on, she had a new Lord, a new love and a new life. As for Simeon, well the Lord, it seems, had no more to say to him.

THREE RICH MEN
LUKE 18:18-30;12:16-21;16:19-31

This is the story of three rich men. It could be that the references are all to the same person, at different stages in his career. Luke tells us about all three. Three words sum up the story of this individual—Too much! Too hard! Too late! We see him as a young man, as a middle-aged man and as a dead man.

When we first meet this man, he is young, rich and eager, and a very likable man. We are told that Jesus looked at him and loved him. Of course, Jesus loves all people; but here was a special case, like that of Martha, Mary and Lazarus and like that of John, "the disciple whom Jesus loved." The young man had everything. He was <u>rich</u>. He was <u>respected</u> for, like Nicodemus, he was a ruler of the Jews. He was <u>religious</u> and even

143

claimed to have kept God's commandments. He was <u>restive</u>. He was aware that there was something lacking in his life, and he came to Jesus to find out what it was. He found out, soon enough. You love your neighbor as yourself, do you? Well, prove it. Sell all you have and share it with the poor. You love God with all your heart, do you? Then prove it. Come and follow Me to Calvary. The Lord was asking for <u>too much</u>. He turned away. The price was too high.

The second glimpse we get of him, he has a problem. His fields had produced bumper crops. What was he to do with all his goods? Help the poor? Not him! That thought never occurred to him. He was <u>too hard</u>. He would build bigger and better barns, that was his proposal. He would store the grain until prices went up in the winter or until a drought year sent grain prices soaring. More! He would enjoy himself, he would have fun, he would eat, drink and be merry.

The plight of the poor did not interest him. He had proved that already when, as a rich young ruler he had come to Christ, claimed to have kept the commandments only to be exposed to the fact that he had no real feeling for the poor and disadvantaged. By now he was <u>too hard</u>. He had cultivated an attitude of total indifference to the poor, even to the poor fellow who haunted the gate of his mansion. Complaisantly he settled down for the night, satisfied with himself. He composed himself to sleep. Little did he know what a fool he was. A voice rang out in the darkness. He would be dead before sunrise. "This night thy soul shall be required of thee, then whose would all those things be?"

We are given one last look at the man. Now he is in a lost eternity. He had allowed a beggar to starve to death at his gate. Now he was dead himself. He was in hell and he was still very much alive. He could see and hear and feel. He could reason and remember. Moreover, he was in torment. He tried to <u>pray</u>. He begged for some alleviation of his sufferings, but his request was denied. It was <u>too late</u>. Praying time was over. There was easy access to God on earth. But no access at all in hell. There was "a great gulf" fixed.

He wanted to <u>preach</u>. "I have five brothers," he said. "Send Lazarus to them. They know Lazarus. They passed him often enough by my gate when they came to my house." His request was denied. "They have Moses and the prophets," he was told. "They have the Bible." "But they don't believe it, and they won't read it," the man cried, "but they would believe a man risen from the dead!" "If they will not believe the Bible, neither will they believe if one were to be raised from the dead," he was told. And that was that. It was too late.

Interestingly enough, the next man Jesus raised from the dead was a man named <u>Lazarus</u> (John 11). So stubborn was the unbelief of the Jewish leaders, they actually tried to put Lazarus back to death (John 12). The Lord was right. Though one arose from the dead they would not believe.

That remains true to this day. One of the best documented and best proved facts of history is the resurrection of Christ from the dead. Hundreds saw Him. His resurrection was public knowledge. The testimony of the four gospels would be accepted as true in any court of law if put to the test using the same laws of evidence used in our courts today.

But will they believe? To this day thousands reject or ignore the fact that Jesus arose from the dead. How terribly sad.

I MUST SEE ROME
ROMANS 1:10-13

Paul had never been to Rome. The church in that great city had been founded by Jews converted under Peter's preaching on the day of Pentecost. Peter should have written to the Romans. But he didn't. Peter was a big man in Jerusalem, but it took a much bigger man to write to Rome.

Although Paul had never been to Rome, he had an intense interest in the place. Indeed, some of his converts were there. Doubtless his fame had already reached the church at Rome because news and information traveled fast on the great highways of the empire. Scraps of truth from his preaching and his pen had likely already reached Rome. Echoes of the controversy against him, stirred up by the legalists, had doubtless also reached the capital. He himself wanted to come there. He decided to write to the Roman Church. Naturally he began by introducing himself. He says three things about himself and his longing for Rome.

He begins with HIS DIVINE AUTHORITY. He was a <u>servant</u>, he says, a slave, a bondslave of Jesus Christ. No man valued his freedom more than Paul. "I was free born," he declared to Claudius Lysias. Just the same he was the willing slave of Christ. When in prison he never regarded his chains as the bonds of Caesar. They were "his bonds in Christ," the badge of his total commitment to the Lord.

He was an <u>apostle</u>, the equal of Peter, James and John. He was God's sent one, with all the power and authority of an apostle and with the gentile world as his field.

And he was "<u>separated</u>." He was separated by God <u>before his birth</u>. He was separated by Christ <u>at his conversion</u>. He was separated by the Holy Spirit <u>at his commissioning</u> for world evangelism (Gal.1:15; Acts 9:15; Acts 13:2). He was armed with authority from God.

Then there was HIS DEFINITE AMBITION. He wanted to go to Rome. He had put "<u>Rome</u>" at the top of his proposed itinerary every time he set out on another crusade. But God had always held him back. Now he signs a blank check. He asks God to write in the amount, no matter what the cost, for him to go to Rome. "By any means!" he says. Not long afterwards, God filled in the amount and sent Paul to Rome, in chains. Paul never complained about that. At least he was in Rome and able to reach out from there.

Finally there was HIS DOCTRINAL ARGUMENT. He mentions the <u>supremacy</u> of the gospel: "I am not ashamed of the gospel," he says. The gospel dealt with facts superior to anything known to Greek logic; with a force superior to all Rome's legions; and with a faith superior to anything known to Jewish light.

Paul proclaimed that Gospel everywhere—in Jerusalem, the religious capital of the world, in Athens, the intellectual capital of the world, and in Rome, the imperial capital of the world. At Jerusalem he was mobbed, at Athens he was mocked and at Rome he was martyred. But still the gospel reigned supreme.

He mentions, moreover, the <u>sufficiency</u> of the gospel. It stirs the mind, it satisfies the heart, it subdues the will, it searches the conscience, it saves the soul and it sanctifies the life. "It is the power of God unto salvation," Paul said.

And he mentions the simplicity of the gospel. It is "to everyone that believeth." All it calls for is simple, childlike trust in God whose word is sacred and can never be broken. Simple? Yes, indeed!

> *"A little child of seven,*
> *Or even three or four,*
> *Can enter into heaven,*
> *Through Christ the open door."*

Simple? Yes! But also sublime. Mark the weighty words Paul uses in his introduction alone: Gospel, Christ, Power, God, Salvation, Everyone, Believeth, Jew, Gentile, Righteousness, Revealed, Faith, Just, and Live. There is enough truth in those fourteen words to occupy our minds for a lifetime!

"I must see Rome!" Paul said. God kept him waiting, because, except for Jerusalem Rome was the most dangerous place in the world for Paul. Besides, it would be good for the gospel, for the churches and for Christians in Rome to have an inspired epistle to prepare them for this intrepid apostle.

THE INNKEEPER OF BETHLEHEM

It was known as Chimham's Inn, and it was hard by Bethlehem. It had been there for a thousand years. The prophet Jeremiah knew about it in his day. It was a well-known place and was about to become the most famous inn in the world.

Caesar Augustus had set the whole world in motion. From the Danube to the Nile, from the tin islands of Britain to the mountains of the moon. From the Euphrates to the Pillars of Hercules, men were on the move, driven by an imperial decree. It paid no heed to anyone's age or condition. It simply forced them to journey to their ancestral homes to be taxed. The carpenter of Nazareth and his wife were thus forced to go to Bethlehem.

Doubtless this journey was contrary to what they had planned with a child on the way. The journey must have been hard and tiring for Mary and an anxious time for her husband. They arrived in the little town of Bethlehem at last, the city of David; and there (as Micah had foretold some seven hundred years before) the Christ was born. Think of it! The Creator of the universe in a barn, of all places, with manure for carpeting, cobwebs for curtains and bats to fly His honor guard.

For there was no room for them in the inn. In the first place, when Joseph and Mary arrived, the innkeeper was busy. The place was packed to the doors. People were paying outrageous prices for a corner in which to spread a bedroll. All about the innkeeper, people were clamoring for food, for wine, for fodder for their camels, for water. The innkeeper and his helpers were rushed off their feet. Supplies had to be fetched from neighboring farms. The innkeeper had to be here, there and everywhere, dealing with salesmen, keeping an eye on the kitchen, harrying the maids, taking in the cash, entertaining his guests.

Joseph was just another interruption. A peasant! A Galilean peasant, a pregnant wife and a donkey! And from despised Nazareth, too, if the innkeeper were any judge of accents. "NO! There is NO room. No room, don't you understand? The place is full. You should have made reservations. I'm sorry about your wife, but that's your problem, not mine."

It is not too hard to picture Joseph, driven to it, perhaps, by desperation, turning on the innkeeper. "Look here, Mr. Innkeeper. I don't expect you to know who we are. I am Joseph, a direct descendent of David, through the line of Solomon. My wife is also a descendent of David through the collateral line of Nathan, Solomon's brother. The Child that is about to be born is rightful heir to David's usurped throne. You can't allow Him to be born on the street." The innkeeper said: "Alright, use the cattle shed," and went back to his work.

And thus it was that the Lord of glory arrived on planet Earth by way of a virgin's womb and was born in a barn and laid in a manger. While men slept and angels sang and the innkeeper retired to his bed and went to sleep to snore his way through the miracle of miracles that took place that night in his barn the Son of God became the Son of Man so that the sons of men might become the sons of God.

The innkeeper of Bethlehem has gone down in history. God kindly withholds his name. All we know about him was that he had no room for Jesus. Mind you, he had a perfectly good room in his inn he could have given to Jesus—his own. The best room in the inn. He never thought of giving that up. What a sad way to be remembered—as the man who had no room for the Son of God.

PHILEMON AND ONESIMUS
PHILEMON 1:1-25

Colossae was a small, sleepy market town on the Wolf River a hundred miles from Ephesus. Once, a busy enough place on the main East-West road, time had passed it by. It is famous now only because Paul wrote a letter to the church in town. Philemon, a wealthy citizen of Colossae, had become a Christian through the ministry of Paul. Perhaps he had met Paul at Ephesus. We do not know. But Philemon, his wife and his son were leading members of the Colossian church.

Onesimus was his slave. Doubtless Philemon was a good enough master, but Onesimus coveted his freedom. For the lot of a slave, at best, was subject to the whim of his owner. He could be scourged or sold or slaughtered. He had no rights. He was just a piece of property. The name Onesimus means "Profitable." But he certainly was not profitable to Philemon. He robbed him and then ran for refuge to Rome. There he could hide from the one to whom he belonged. He is a type and picture of all of us, runaways from God.

The slums of Rome, Onesimus thought, would be a perfect hiding place; but he reckoned without God. Somehow he ran into Paul who, though a prisoner, had considerable liberty and his own hired house.

"Ah! Onesimus! What are you doing here?" we can almost hear Paul say. The long and the short of it was that Paul led Onesimus to Christ. "And now, my friend," he said, "we'll have to send you back." The least Onesimus could expect was to be scourged. The law allowed him to be crucified. Custom and the law would all be on the slave owner's side, and other slave owners would expect Philemon to be severe. Leniency to a runaway slave was rare. Onesimnus was alarmed. "I'll be your mediator," said Paul. "You don't belong to me. You belong to another. Back you must go, no matter what." It was no cheap gospel that was preached in those days.

So Onesimus went back to Philemon, but he was not expected to plead his own case. Paul gave him a memo to be given to his master. Perhaps he read it to him: "Onesimus," he wrote, "is my child . . . my very heart. If thou countest me as a partner, receive him as myself . . ." Paul did not ask that Onesimus be received back as a slave, but as though he were Paul himself. How would Philemon have received Paul? Would he have put him back there in the slave compound? Never! He would have killed for him the fatted calf, sat him in the seat of honor at his table, put him in the guest room and crowned him with glory and honor.

Philemon might well have balked. Onesimus had stolen money from him. "Put that to my account," said Paul, as our Mediator says to God. "As for the future good behavior of your returned slave, well, all I can say is that from now on, if it's a <u>slave</u> you want, you'll find him up to his name, profitable indeed."

But there was more to it than that. He was now "a brother beloved." Calvary abolishes all class distinction between believers. It puts master and man on the same footing.

So Onesimus said "Goodbye" to Paul and, clutching this memo tightly in his hand, headed back to the one to whom he belonged. The story is a perfect little gem. The only thing that stood between him and a cross was a mediator back there in Rome. And a memorandum of less than 140 words.

We do not know how Onesimus was received. Paul, however, had no doubts. In the epistle he wrote to the Colossians about this time or soon after, he mentions Onesimus. He refers to him as "a faithful and beloved brother who is one of you" (Col.4:9). And can we doubt it? Though Paul organized no marches or demonstrations, this memo of his struck a blow against slavery and for freedom unsurpassed.

THE PRAYERS OF THE PRODIGAL
LUKE 15:12,19

The prodigal son had two prayers. First, there was HIS GOING AWAY PRAYER: "Father, give me!" It was a wicked, selfish prayer, the prayer of a young hippie tired of restraint and tired of religion. He was tired, too, of his relations, his father who reigned him in, and his brother who ran him down. Indeed, one can feel sorry for any boy who has an older brother like the prodigal's—a smug, self-satisfied hypocrite and snob. It would be enough to make any one with red blood in his veins run away. That Pharasaical elder brother of his made the world and its ways very attractive to the prodigal son.

So the prodigal responded to the <u>call of the world</u>. The far country beckoned, all smiles and good cheer. It offered freedom from all the restrictions of a godly home. It offered a wide gate and a broad highway where sin was called by other, friendlier names.

He responded, too, to <u>the congratulations of the world</u>. He headed for the far country with plenty of money in his pocket. He had youth and charm and he paid generously for all his fair-weather friends to have their fun. So, for as long as his money lasted, it was wine, women and song, a fast life and plenty of laughs. But then his money ran out. At once the world turned a different face towards him.

He began to learn something of <u>the cares of this world</u>. A famine arose and even capable, local men were thrown out of work. He felt the pinch of poverty. He was hungry. Nobody gave him so much as a dime. His fast-living friends abandoned him. He was out of work and out of money and far from home. He was lonely and hungry and cold.

He learned, too, in that far country, in Corinth, perhaps, or Athens, or Rome, or where ever it was he went, something of <u>the coldness of the world</u>. Gone were its smiles, gone was its song. He stood amid busy, bustling throngs and starved. "He joined himself," Jesus said, "to a citizen of that country," but starvation wages was all he could earn. And what a job it was! He was hired to feed swine. What depths of disgrace for a well-born Jew! Feeding swine! Worse still, he became so hungry that he ate the slops in the pig pail, and starved. So much for his going away prayer.

Now comes his COMING HOME PRAYER: No longer, Father <u>give</u> me," but, "Father <u>make</u> me, make me as one of thy hired servants." His father's servants lived like lords of the land, well-housed, well-paid, well-dressed, well-fed—while he perished with hunger. "He came to himself," Jesus said. And then he came to the father. "I am no more worthy to be called thy son," he said. "Make me as one of your hired servants."

We can picture the boy as he bangs on the door of the big house on the hill in that faraway land. "Here, Mister, here's your pig pail, and thanks for nothing. I'm going home to my father." The man would look him up and down with scorn, taking in his unwashed body, his unkempt beard, the marks of dissipation on his face. "Well, boy," he would say, "more the fool you are. If I were your father, I'd set the dogs on you." And the boy would say: "I daresay you would, but you don't know my father."

Nor did the prodigal for that matter. When he finally arrived home, it was not the servant's hall to which he was sent. He was caught in the father's embrace. The robe and the ring and the fatted calf were his, and new life. And the whole priceless story, from the lips of the Lord, a parable of God's dealings with us.

WALKING ON THE WAVES
MATTHEW 14:22-23

He had never done it before. He would never do it again. But for one glorious, dizzy moment, Peter walked upon the waves. And they felt solid as cement, even while they moved like a roller coaster beneath his feet. If he didn't look at them, he was alright. It took him a moment to get his balance and get the hang of how to walk on a moving platform, but he did it. And thereon hangs a tale. We really have three pictures to examine here.

First, there is a picture of PERIL. It had been a most remarkable day of sublime teaching, teaching that touched the heart and stirred the soul. But, secretly, everyone had hoped for a miracle, just one would do, for now! And what a miracle it was when it came! There was the Lord, and there was the lad, and there were the loaves. A small boy's little lunch, magnanimously given to the Master. And suddenly there was bread enough and to spare to feed upwards of ten thousand hungry people! No wonder everyone wanted to crown Him King, then and there! The Lord, however, quickly defused that package of high explosive. He sent the disciples away first because they were as excited as the rest. Then He stayed behind to quietly and efficiently dismiss the cheering multitudes.

"You fellows go on ahead. I'll meet you on the other side," He said. So off they went and, soon afterwards, evening twilight faded; and the darkness came. What a position! To be adrift on life's tempestuous sea, without Christ, and in the dark. But darkness was followed by danger. A storm came, and what a storm! The disciples, many of them old hands at sailing that lake, knew how dangerous a storm on Galilee could be. They were in peril, and they knew it.

But there was something they had forgotten, they were in the center of the Lord's will. His <u>intention put</u> them in that place of peril. His <u>intercession preserved</u> them in that place of peril. They were in the safest place on earth, in the very center of His will for them, right there, right then.

The next picture is one of PANIC. They were paralyzed with fear. The wind howled and the waves heaved, and the little ship was tossed about. Then they saw it, way out over the water, a human form climbing the crests of the wild waves and negotiating the deepest troughs. A ghost! After all, this was a demon-haunted lake. On its shores Christ had cast out many evil spirits. The disciples cried out in terror. Then came His cheerful hail: "It is I! Be not afraid!" Their terror fled. Jesus had come.

Which brings us to a picture of PETER, impulsive, impetuous Peter! Look at his <u>desire</u>. His desire was to walk upon those waves, to be like Jesus, to be with Jesus. Bravo, Simon Peter!

Notice also his <u>decision</u>. The Lord called to him to come. He flung his feet over the side and placed them on the nearest wave and let go! It was the bravest thing he ever did before Pentecost. Well done, Peter!

Note also his <u>despair</u>. One step, two steps. He could hardly believe it. Then, for a moment, distracted by the storm, he took his eyes off Jesus—and sank! "<u>Lord</u>," he cried, "<u>save me</u>!" It is the gospel in three words. And saved he was!

Come to think of it, that was the best thing that could have happened. Apart from that sudden despair, Peter might have boasted afterwards about his experience. He might have started a cult. A defeat which leaves us humble is better than a victory which leaves us proud.

DOCTOR LUKE
COLOSSIANS 4:14; PHILEMON 24; II TIMOTHY 4:11

Luke is mentioned only three times in the New Testament. He was a Greek. Possibly he was "the man from Macedonia" who walked into the missionary's camp at Troas, after Paul's midnight dream, and turned Paul's steps toward Europe.

We recognize him as A VERY BRILLIANT MAN. We are indebted to him for what he tells us about the Christ. Luke's gospel has been called "the most beautiful book in the world." It was probably written during the period of Paul's imprisonment at Caesarea, possibly during his imprisonment at Rome. Luke had access to many of the people concerned, and he had a thorough knowledge of the facts. Doubtless he would often confer with Paul about various facts he was investigating. His gospel is rich in stories of human interest. He records six miracles and nineteen parables mentioned nowhere else, including the Good Samaritan, the Prodigal Son and the Rich Fool. Such Pauline words as faith, repentance, mercy and forgiveness show up often.

Then, too, we are indebted to Luke for what he tells us about the Church. The book of Acts, written by Luke, forms an essential bridge between the gospels and the epistles. With consummate skill, and from a thorough acquaintance with the facts, Luke traces the early history of the church from an upper room in Jerusalem to a prison house in Rome. He weaves his story around the personalities of Simon, Stephen and Saul. He points out the founding emphasis, the forward emphasis and the foreign emphasis of the church and leaves the story dangling, incomplete and unfinished. Countless other chapters, covering some two thousand years of time, would yet need to be written; but that was far beyond the scope of even Luke's busy pen.

Then, too, Luke was A VERY BELOVED MAN. He was one of Paul's dearest and closest friends. Paul was not a well man. When we think of the beatings, the scourgings, the shipwrecks, the imprisonment's, the dangers he had endured, it is little wonder he needed the constant attendance of a physician. When Paul finally arrived back in Philippi, where Luke lived, after having gone through some of the horrendous experiences he describes in 2 Corinthians, Luke doubtless insisted on giving his friend a thorough overhaul. "That does it, Paul," we can hear him say, "from now on, I'm traveling with you." The "beloved physician," Paul calls him.

Finally, he was A VERY BRAVE MAN. When Paul appealed to Caesar in A.D. 59, to escape the peril he was in at the hands of the Jewish and Roman authorities, Nero had not yet shown his true colors. But times changed for the worse. In A.D. 64 Nero set fire to Rome and blamed the Christians, and a nightmare persecution broke out. Paul was remanded back to prison. Not, this time, to his own hired house and the privileges secured by his Roman citizenship, but to the so-called Steps of Groaning and into the dreaded Mammertime Prison. There he was stripped and lowered into the terrible lower dungeon, the infamous Tullianum. There to await death. Some of his colleagues he sent away. Some, like Demas, abandoned him. Only his beloved Doctor Luke remained.

One morning the executioners came for Paul. Doubtless the daring doctor accompanied him to the place of death. His head was struck from his shoulders. His soul soared upwards to glory, and Luke disappears. But we shall hear more about this brave man one of these days, at the judgment seat of Christ, when the full tale will be told; and Jesus will be heard to say: "Well done, Luke! Well done."

Solomon's Three Books: Song Of Solomon

Song Of Solomon 1:3

It is not at all surprising that Solomon became the author of three of the best selling books in the world. The books reflect different states in his remarkable career. One book records his great <u>disappointment</u>, one well deserved and the inevitable result of his own lustful lifestyle. The second book illustrates his great <u>discernment</u>, the genius he had for reducing great truths to simple sayings. The final book demonstrates the great <u>disparity</u> so sadly evident between what he taught and what he wrought.

First, we consider <u>The Song of Solomon</u>. This is a <u>**BOOK OF ROMANCE**</u>. It is a love song, one in which Solomon was inspired by the Holy Spirit to tell us about the one woman he could not have. She turned him down, despite all his efforts to turn her thoughts and desires to him.

It is often claimed that in the Song of Solomon, Solomon is a type of Christ. How can that be? He <u>is</u> a type of Christ in respect to the <u>kingdom</u>, for when Christ comes back, He will reign as David, putting down all His foes; and then He will reign as Solomon in prosperity, peace and power. Solomon's personal life, however, was a national scandal. He came very close to apostasy and did more than any other king to undermine and eventually destroy the kingdom of Israel. Look, for instance, at Solomon's proposal to the Shulamite! "I have sixty wives," he said, "and another eighty women I am living with. Indeed, I have more women that I can count, but you can be first" (6:8). Who can put such words into the mouth of the pure and holy Jesus?

There is <u>another</u>, however, who plays out his part in this song of songs, a beloved shepherd, to whom the Shulamite has already given her heart. Solomon exerts all his personal charm, his way with words, his position, his power, his ability to gratify desires for worldly success in order to awe and win the Shulamite. If Solomon is a type of anyone in this book, it is the prince of this world who would seduce us from Christ as Solomon tried to turn away the Shulamite's affections from her beloved shepherd to himself. Indeed, this is the real key to the book.

Though abducted by Solomon to his pavilion, and though courted ardently by Solomon, and though exposed to the urgings of Solomon's other women, women who had surrendered to his personality, promises and passion, the Shulamite remained true to her absent beloved.

Her final rejection of Solomon's overtures is classic and it gives us the key to overcoming temptation. "I am my beloved's" she said, "and his desire is towards me." Note that! She did not say "<u>my</u> desire is towards him" (though, of course, that was perfectly true), but "<u>his</u> desire is towards me." Solomon had no more to say.

Surely, that should be our stand in temptation's hour. "I am my Beloved's and HIS desire is towards ME." Think of it! The desire of the Lord Himself, the King of glory, Creator of the universe, the One whom angels worship, is towards ME!" Wonder of wonders! Surely no temptation can be successful in the face of the wonder of that. It is only when we forget this marvelous truth that temptation has its way.

THE SONG OF SOLOMON (2)
SONG OF SOLOMON 5:10-16

The book begins with an hour of trouble. The Shulamite, having been abducted into Solomon's pavilion in the country, finds herself virtually a prisoner. She calls out to her absent shepherd. She longs for his love. She delights to speak his name. The daughters of Jerusalem, who love the lustful Solomon, overhear her and alarm her.

Then Solomon comes. He flatters her and makes all kinds of promises to her, offering her silver and gold in exchange for her love. Then he hurries off to a banquet, satisfied he has made a good impression, one he can exploit at a later date.

But he is mistaken. The Shulamite's beloved shepherd comes to where she is, confined in Solomon's country pavilion, and she and her shepherd exchange endearments. She describes his desired rustic table and contrasts it with Solomon's loaded board.

This hour of tenderness ends, and the court women reappear. They try to stir up the Shulamite's passion, hoping it can be used to snare her. Their goal is to detach her affections from her shepherd and to seduce her into making an alliance with the worldly prince Solomon. They do not succeed. She sharply rebukes them and tells them not to incite her desires. She gives them her testimony. She tells how once she thought that she had lost her beloved. Though it was night time, she had gone to look for him, only to be frightened by the night watchmen. Thankfully, however, she found her shepherd. "I held him," she says, "and would not let him go."

Solomon, tiring of the country, now decided to return to Jerusalem. He approached the city, carrying along the Shulamite in a closed carriage. The way was lined by his admiring subjects. They make comments about him. They praise his worldly passions, and his power, his possessions and his exalted position. They comment on the spectacle of the impressive imperial guard marching beside the king. They talk about his marriage to the queen and recall how he had been crowned by his mother on that occasion.

Although she is now a prisoner, the Shulamite manages to arrange another meeting with her shepherd. He says to her, "Thou art all fair, my love." She tells him that all that she has is his.

Solomon's court women reappear and the Shulamite tells them of a dream she once had. In her dream her beloved came, but she had been too lazy to respond so he had gone away. She had run after him, only to find herself again in trouble with the watchmen. Thankfully, it was only a dream. She describes to the women the beauty of her beloved, and they want to know how they can find him. Suddenly suspicious of their motives, she refuses to tell them.

Now Solomon comes back, armed with flatteries. His words are distressingly frank and brazen. His description of her charms are daring and distressful. The Shulamite, however, is arrayed in the armour of her goodness, and he does not dare to touch her, powerful as he is. Through it all, she remains true to her beloved. "I am my beloved's," she said, "and his desire is towards me." Solomon, silenced and defeated, lets her go. He failed to achieve his goal of winning her away from her shepherd.

The book ends with two last requests. The shepherd pleads with his beloved Shulamite to let him hear her voice. The Shulamite pleads with the shepherd to come soon and receive her unto himself.

When viewed thus, the Song of Solomon teaches us how to overcome the wiles of the prince of this world and how to be victorious and true to our Beloved when exposed to the snares of this world.

SOLOMON'S THREE BOOKS: PROVERBS
PROVERBS 2:12,16

The Queen of Sheba came from distant shores to sit at Solomon's feet. Across the dreary dunes of the desert up the long reaches of the Nile on into the hill country of Judah, there to drink deep of the wise man's wonderful words. For the fame of Solomon's wisdom was heralded far and wide. This wisdom of his was not for his generation alone. Solomon was inspired of God to write it down. Under the guidance of the Holy Spirit

Solomon reduced his insights regarding government, psychology and natural history, into homespun proverbs, witty sayings which capsulize truth and make it easy to remember.

The sacred historian tells us that Solomon wrote three thousand proverbs, of which only about a third have survived. Some take the pithy proverbs of this book to be promises as, for instance, the one which says: "Train up a child in the way he should go, and when he is old he will not depart from it." But that and similar proverbs are not unconditional <u>promises</u>, they state <u>principles</u>. For that is what the proverbs of Solomon are, principles to live by.

The proverbs of Solomon fall into three categories. The first nine chapters deal with MORAL issues. Solomon personifies wisdom as a woman, standing at life's crossroads, pleading with those who pass by to come and sample her wares. He contrasts this pure and lovely woman with the adulteress and harlot. In one of his graphic pictorial passages, Solomon tells how he watched from his window as a woman of the world won a youthful wanderer to her lusts. It is a sad commentary on Solomon's own moral torpidity that he made no attempt to warn the lad or to stop the woman. He should have put her to death. He seems to have been well versed in her persuasive powers. At least he tells us just what she said. His attitude, as he watched the drama unfold beneath his eyes, seems to have been one of detached philosophical interest. It was just another entry in his case book (Prov. 7:6-27).

In the next nine or ten chapters, he deals with MISCELLANEOUS issues, comparing and contrasting the lifestyles of the godly person on the one hand and the godless on the other. "Fools make a mock at sin," he says. "There is a way that seemeth right unto a man," he says, "but the end thereof are the ways of death." We recognize scores of such sayings.

The rest of the book deals with MONARCHICAL issues, advice given to those who are in authority. "Take away the wicked from before the king, and his throne shall be established in righteousness," he says. "When the wicked are multiplied, transgression increaseth." We see these deathless principles at work in our own land.

The trouble with Solomon was that he never took his own advice. What he <u>was</u> spoke so loudly that his son, Rehoboam, never listened to a word he said. Who was the greater fool? Solomon or his son?

We can be grateful Jesus says: "A greater than Solomon is here." He Himself was wisdom incarnate—and He practiced what He preached.

SOLOMON'S THREE BOOKS: ECCLESIASTES

Solomon wrote one book when he was young, a book of romance, a second book in his middle age, a book of rules, and a final book when he was old, a book of regrets. That book we call "Ecclesiastes." In it Solomon reflects on the course and consequences of a misspent life. He addresses it to young people, doubtless in the hope that they will not repeat his own follies.

God had visited Solomon on two occasions and loaded him with blessings and benefits. He visited him a third time in wrath. It was not so much his lustful lifestyle, for Solomon was able to more or less legalize his lust by marrying the women he wanted. It was his toleration for the foul and fierce pagan gods of his wives and his actual worship of them, which brought down God's wrath upon his head.

Stunned, Solomon pondered his follies and then took up his pen. The text for his long sermon was doubtless taken from Psalm 39. His topic was the vanity of man "under the sun"—the vanity, emptiness and folly of living as though there was no end to life, no God in heaven and no world but this one. The book is a sermon based on Solomon's experiences as a backslider, his belated repentance and his inadequate conclusions about life. "Vanity" can be written across a life lived without God, a life dominated by the things of time and sense. Roughly paraphrased, the word can be rendered "chasing the wind."

Solomon tells us of some of the things he had SOUGHT. He drew on a wide experience of life because he had gone in for everything "under the sun." To begin with, he had tried the world of thought. Surely the answer to life was to become an intellectual and have people come to you to drink in your wisdom. When he achieved success and fame along this line, it left him unsatisfied. Next, he tried the world of thrills and abandoned himself to pleasure. He sought to gratify the flesh and enjoy the world. Satiated with pleasure he gave up that pursuit as being insane. Finally, he tried the world of things and sought joy in making money. Soon he had everything money could buy, but nothing satisfied and he actually ended up contemplating suicide. "I hated life," he said.

Next Solomon tells us of the things he had <u>seen</u>. Everywhere he looked it was the same sad story, nothing satisfied. He had been living for time and for the things of time. He belatedly discovered that "God has set eternity in the heart." He was like the modern corporate executive who had reached the top of the ladder—only to discover it was up against the wrong wall.

Finally, Solomon tells us of the things he had <u>studied</u>. He became increasingly cynical, especially about women. And no wonder! His palace must have been a pandemonium of jealousy, spite and intrigue, thanks to the thousand women he kept in his harem.

Worse still, Solomon was haunted by the fear of death. He mentions it more and more. He dreaded death and hated growing old.

In the last two chapters Solomon finally emerged from the fog and began to look beyond and above the sun. And there was God! God hadn't moved! <u>He</u>, Solomon, was the one who had moved. Now he had to come back to God to face judgment for his misspent life. It was a frightening thought.

In the end, he wrote his book. The Holy Spirit enabled him to do so and gave him this last chance to make amends. And so, no doubt, he has, for people have been reading his warnings in Ecclesiastes for nearly three thousand years. And surely many have been warned.

MARTHA, MARY AND LAZARUS

Martha was a <u>worker</u>. The death, burial and resurrection of Lazarus profoundly changed her attitude toward serving the Lord and His people. Before, she had been critical of Mary. No longer! She had buried her touchiness in the grave of Lazarus. Now she served as one on resurrection ground.

Mary was a <u>worshipper</u>. She was always at Jesus' feet, listening attentively to the Lord's words. She had one prized possession, a flask of very expensive perfume. Perhaps she had kept it in her room against the day of her wedding or, failing that, the day of her burial. Listening to Jesus changed her mind. It dawned on her that Jesus was soon going to <u>die</u>. He would need ointment for <u>His</u> burying. She said nothing but, from then on, treasured up that costly perfume for <u>Him</u>. Doubtless she had been put under considerable pressure by Martha to give it for the burying of Lazarus. She refused, much as she loved her brother. She kept it. Jesus said, "against the day of my burying hath she kept this."

Then something else took hold of her heart. At the time the Lord raised Lazarus, He declared Himself to be "the resurrection and the life." Mary seized on that. "So," she said to herself, "He'll really not need this ointment for His <u>burying</u> after all. He's going to rise again. I'll not wait until He's dead. The next time He comes, I'll give it to Him then." And so she did.

Lazarus, of course, was a <u>witness</u>. He had been a believer for some time, one of Jesus' closest friends. His home had long been a gathering place for those who loved the Lord. Everyone knew that. But the fact that he was a believer did not much interest people. Nobody beat a path to his door to see him just because he was a believer.

But look at them now. We read, "Much people of the Jews came—that they might see Lazarus . . . whom He (Jesus) had raised from the dead." They are coming in droves. What made the difference? Resurrection! There is something wonderfully attractive about someone living a resurrected life.

Suppose we were to ask Lazarus: "What is the secret of this new life of yours?" He would say: "I was always a devout believer, you know. But one day I died. I died to my family, to my career, to my opinions—to everything. I was very dead indeed. You don't expect much from a dead man. Martha knew I was dead. 'By this time he stinketh,' she said. She was right. All you can do with a dead man is bury him."

"Then Jesus came. I had come to an utter end of myself. Jesus gave me new life—resurrection life. I am not the same Lazarus you used to know. That Lazarus died. Now 'I live, yet not I but Christ liveth in me.' I am a witness to what Christ can do with a dead man, I am a living epistle, known and read of all men. I am not <u>trying</u> to be a witness, you understand, I don't go out knocking on doors. I don't hand out tracts. I didn't take a course on soul winning. I just live a resurrected life, that's all. God does the rest."

And the people come. One suspects they would still come if we would live resurrected lives.

MUCH MORE

"Much more!" says Paul. He says it five times in a row. Behind the statement can be seen the shadow of the Old Testament trespass offering. Before the transgressor could offer his trespass offering, he had to restore fully what he had stolen, plus a penalty of an additional twenty percent (Lev.5:16). Thus the wronged party actually became the gainer!

As a result of man's sin and God's salvation, we become the gainers. Adam might have lived in Eden in sinless perfection forever, but his posterity would have remained sons of Adam. Now they get much more, they become sons of God.

Moreover, God becomes the gainer. God could demonstrate His wisdom and His power in creation, but it was Calvary that gave Him a platform on which to demonstrate His love. As the old hymn puts it:

> *"God is love we surely know*
> *By our Savior's depths of woe."*

Paul shows us, with his five "much mores," five ways God has been able to demonstrate His love because of Calvary and thus become the gainer. We stand in awe of His wisdom and His power. We are overwhelmed by His love.

First we look at HIS LOVE AND HIS GOVERNMENT: "God commendeth His love toward us in that while we were yet sinners Christ died for us. Much more then, being now justified by His blood we shall be saved from wrath through Him." Think for a moment of that world "justified." The Law can forgive a guilty man, but it cannot justify him. To be forgiven, we must plead "guilty." To be justified, we plead "not guilty." The best God's government, based on His law, can offer the sinner is a fair trial or a free pardon. The death of Christ at Calvary enables God to declare me justified—just-as-if-I'd never sinned. Justification puts us beyond the reach of God's wrath. But at what a cost!

We think next of HIS LOVE AND HIS GOODNESS: "For if when we were enemies we were reconciled to God by the death of His Son, much more, being reconciled we shall be saved by His life." The Lord's goodness was absolute goodness, not relative goodness. It qualified Him to die on our behalf. He was like the Old Testament sacrificial lamb, without spot or blemish. Christ died so we could escape the penalty of sin. But there is much more. He who gave His life <u>for me</u>, to save me from the penalty of sin, now gives His life <u>to me</u>, so that I can escape the <u>power of sin</u>.

Next we contemplate HIS LOVE AND HIS GIFT: "But not as the offense, so also is the free gift. For if through the offense of one many be dead, <u>much more</u> the grace of God and the gift by grace, which is by one man, Jesus Christ, hath abounded unto many." The first Adam bequeathed death on his children. That was <u>his</u> gift to us. <u>God's</u> gift is "eternal life through Jesus Christ our Lord." God in His superlative love, does not just give us back natural life, He gives eternal life.

We think too of HIS LOVE AND HIS GLORY: "For if by one man's offense death reigned by one, <u>much more</u> they which receive abundance of grace and of the gift of righteousness shall reign in life by one, Jesus Christ." Again God demonstrates the superlative nature of His love. We, who were once rebels, are now destined for the throne, to be seated with Christ in the highest heaven, above principalities and powers and every name which is named, not only in this life, but also in the life to come. We will reign with Him on high!

Finally, we think of HIS LOVE AND HIS GRACE: "But where sin abounded, grade did <u>much more</u> abound." Well might John Newton sing:

> *"Amazing grace how sweet the sound*
> *That saved a wretch like me;*
> *I once was lost, but now am found*
> *Was blind, but now I see."*

So, then, Calvary is the stage upon which God demonstrates His love. And we, the objects of that love, will be exhibited eternally as its trophies, to the admiration and wonder of all the angel throng.